SALADS AND *Sips*

Mixing it up with

THE BELHAVEN HOUSE AND GARDEN CLUB

Queens' Press

JACKSON, MISSISSIPPI

Copies of Salads & Sips may be ordered at
    Amazon.com
    BarnesandNoble.com
    CreateSpace.com/3953059
For wholesale inquiries,
contact CreateSpace Direct at 866-356-2154

Proceeds from Salads & Sips will benefit the Greater Belhaven
Neighborhood Foundation, *www.greaterbelhaven.com*

Belhaven House & Garden Club Cookbook Committee
Anne Robertson and Carol Taff, editors
Jane Alexander, Barbara Austin, Vidal Blankenstein, Judy Wiener

Cover design by Vidal Blankenstein, *www.imaginarycompany.com*
Interior design by Emily Cavett Taff

Printed in the United States of America.

ISBN-13: 978-0-61-571498-1
ISBN-10: 0-615-71498-6

Table of Contents

INTRODUCTION

Why we love our Garden Club

When my friends hear I am in a garden club, they laugh—because I have a notoriously "brown thumb." So I explain that my garden club is a uniquely Southern institution: *the Garden Club That Doesn't Garden.* We don't discuss plants and flowers and other growing things. Instead, we spend one Tuesday a month during the year (not summers, because summers are just TOO hot to socialize) getting together at a member's home, eating lunch and drinking iced tea or wine. At least once a year we invite our spouses to join us at an evening "happy hour" party, just so they don't forget how to have fun.

We call the president our Queen, and she has the pillow and scepter to prove it. In our club, it really is good to be the queen.

Our first meeting of the year, in September, is traditionally to meet our newest members. Every member brings a salad of some kind, to serve "however many." The salads in this book have found their way to the homes of many members, oozing hospitality (and "real," though rarely homemade, mayonnaise) onto the platter.

One thing you should know: we've been known to go to a lot of trouble to have a party. Every other spring, we used to have Spring Party, which started out as a spring party but morphed into SPRING PARTY, and so, doesn't happen anymore. But the recipes contained in this book include "sips" from these legendary occasions, as well as some favorites of our legendary hostesses (who find "sips" helpful in reaching the proper state of mind to welcome 500 of their closest friends into their home to drink Sangria. Really.)

Something else you should know: It used to be really, really difficult to gain admission to our august ranks. Membership was limited to the number of women one could comfortably seat in one's living room. So basically, someone had to die before a new member could be elected. We're more democratic now, and we have too many members to seat everyone in one room—in most of our houses, anyway. But we have fun! That's the purpose and the mission of our group. Because, while we all do live in a historic neighborhood, and give to good causes and serve on boards and show up at church on Sundays, this is not a club where we DO. This is a club where we just ARE. We are the Belhaven House and Garden Club. And we have FUN.

👑 Jane Clover Alexander

Once a Queen, always a Queen—so we honor them, past and present, by sticking a crown by their names.

The Cookbook Committee

Fruit & Cheese

Apple Sauce and Red Hot Salad	12	Heavenly Salad	14
Beverly's Avocado and Grapefruit Salad	9	Merrill's Avocado and Grapefruit Salad	9
Blueberry and Feta Salad	6	Mississippi Watermelon Salad	5
Cranberry Relish	11	My Sister's Pretzel Salad	16
Eloise's Cottage Cheese	7	Orange Salad Mold	15
Erma's Waldorf Salad	10	Pimento-less Cheese	6
Fall Pear Salad	10	Pineapple Lemon Salad	13
Five-Cup Fruit Salad	11	Prosciutto and Honeydew Salad	4
Frosted Lime Salad	14	Quick Fruit Salad	7
Frozen Fruit Salad	12	Sebelle Salad	16
Grape Salad	8	Strawberry Salad	13
Green Stuff	15	Virginia's Fruit Salad	8
Grilled Peach, Onion and Bacon Salad with Buttermilk Dressing	3	Virginia's Strawberry Salad	4
		Watermelon and Tomato Salad	5

GRILLED PEACH, ONION AND BACON SALAD *with* BUTTERMILK DRESSING

Serves 8

1 pound thick-sliced bacon

¼ cup light brown sugar

½ teaspoon cayenne pepper

3 pounds Vidalia or other sweet onions, cut into
 1-inch thick slabs

extra virgin olive oil, for brushing

4 large ripe peaches, cut into ½-inch wedges

BUTTERMILK DRESSING

¼ cup mayonnaise

¼ cup sour cream

¼ cup buttermilk

2 Tablespoons mint, chopped

2 Tablespoons parsley, chopped

2 Tablespoons chives, snipped

1 teaspoon apple cider vinegar

salt

freshly-ground black pepper

Preheat oven to 325°. In a small bowl, make dressing by whipping the mayonnaise with the sour cream, buttermilk, mint, parsley, chives and vinegar and season with salt and pepper. Refrigerate.

Line a large rimmed baking sheet with parchment paper. Arrange the bacon slices on the sheet in a single layer and sprinkle with the brown sugar and cayenne. Bake for about 25 minutes, until caramelized (the bacon will crisp as it cools). Let cool, then cut the bacon into bite-size pieces.

Meanwhile, light a grill or preheat a grill pan. Brush the onions with olive oil and season with salt and pepper. Grill over moderate heat, turning occasionally, until softened and browned, 10 minutes. Separate the onions into rings. Brush the peaches with olive oil and grill over moderately high heat until tender, 2 minutes. Transfer to a plate.

In a large bowl, toss the onions with the peaches and bacon. Add the buttermilk dressing and toss to coat. Serve right away.

Debbie Cannon from *www.foodandwine.com*

PROSCIUTTO AND HONEYDEW SALAD

Serves 4

- 1 honeydew
- Salt and pepper
- 8 thin slices of prosciutto
- 4-5 cups of arugula, washed, stemmed and patted dry
- extra virgin olive oil
- Parmesan cheese
- ¼ cup Balsamic Syrup

Seed honeydew and cut into 12 wedges, removing rind. Salt and pepper honeydew and wrap two pieces of prosciutto around each wedge. Put arugula in a bowl and toss with olive oil, salt and pepper. Place greens in center on four plates and arrange three pieces of honeydew around the greens on each plate. Shave the Parmesan cheese over the greens. Drizzle Balsamic Syrup over each salad.

BALSAMIC SYRUP
Over medium heat, bring 3 cups balsamic vinegar to a boil and lower the heat. Simmer until the liquid is thickened and reduced to about ¼ cup. This takes about 30 minutes. Cool completely.

Carol Taff

VIRGINIA'S STRAWBERRY SALAD

- 6 cups mixed greens, torn
- 2½ cups sliced strawberries
- 1 cup cheddar cheese
- ½ cup chopped walnuts

DRESSING
- ½ cup vegetable oil
- ⅓ cup sugar
- ¼ cup red wine vinegar
- 1 clove garlic minced
- ¼ teaspoon salt
- ¼ teaspoon paprika
- ⅛ teaspoon black pepper

Mix and refrigerate dressing, then combine with salad ingredients when ready to serve.

Virginia Ezelle

MISSISSIPPI WATERMELON SALAD

3 cups seedless watermelon, cubed

1 seedless cucumber, thinly sliced

½ red onion, thinly sliced

½ cup feta cheese, crumbled

1 cup arugula

5-6 sprigs cilantro

5-6 leaves of fresh mint, chiffonade

2 Tablespoons extra virgin olive oil

2 limes, juiced

salt

pepper

Combine all ingredients in a large bowl and toss. Add salt and pepper to taste. Serve immediately.

Serenity Luckett from Nate Ballard, local Belhaven chef and great friend

WATERMELON AND TOMATO SALAD

1 (3-pound) piece watermelon, remove rind, seeds and cut into ¾-inch chunks

2 large ripe tomatoes, cut into ¾-inch chunks

1 cup feta cheese, crumbled (about 4 ounces)

⅔ cup mint and parsley, chopped (or cilantro and parsley)

2 Tablespoons extra virgin olive oil

1 Tablespoon white balsamic or champagne vinegar

Stir together and season lightly with salt and pepper. Best served shortly after assembled.

Rebecca Wiggs

BLUEBERRY FETA SALAD

3 cups blueberries

2 small cucumbers, peeled, seeds scraped out
and cut into 1-inch pieces on a diagonal

3 scallions, thinly sliced

1 cup crumbled feta

1 heart of romaine, chopped

2 cups mint leaves

DRESSING
4 Tablespoons extra virgin olive oil

4 Tablespoons white wine vinegar

1 Tablespoon honey

salt, to taste

black pepper, to taste

Combine salad ingredients in a large bowl. In a
smaller bowl, whisk together dressing ingredients.
Pour dressing on salad and toss to coat.

Elizabeth Alley

PIMENTO-LESS CHEESE

3 tablespoons red onion, chopped

3 tablespoons cider vinegar

1 teaspoon black pepper

½ teaspoon cayenne pepper

¼ cup Hellman's mayonnaise

4 cups sharp cheddar, shredded

In the bowl of a food processor fitted with regular
blade, pulse to combine first 4 ingredients. Add
mayonnaise. Pulse to combine. Add 4 cups sharp
cheddar cheese. Pulse to combine. If mixture is too
dry, add small amounts of vinegar and mayonnaise
to reach desired consistency.

Stella Gray Sykes

ELOISE'S COTTAGE CHEESE

2 large containers of large curd cottage cheese

1 onion

1 bell pepper

2-3 Tablespoons mayonnaise

5 shots Tabasco

salt

pepper

Place cottage cheese in a colander in the sink and rinse well—let sit to drain, at least 15 minutes, shaking the colander from time to time. The longer it drains the dryer and better the cottage cheese will be. Meanwhile, chop bell pepper and onion into small pieces (think color and texture).

Mix 2 to 3 tablespoons of mayonnaise with 5 big shots of Tabasco—must be Tabasco!

When cottage cheese is drained and fairly dry, mix with mayonnaise mixture and add chopped veggies. Salt to taste. Let it sit for a day if possible—this lasts in the fridge for about a week—the longer it sits the better it gets.

You can use this to stuff a ripe tomato or just eat it with crackers. It is a great complement to a summer supper of veggies. Doubles well. Travels well in a cooler—prepare ahead and take to the beach—a quick meal any time.

Merrill Tenney McKewen via her mom,
Eloise Wilkins Tenney

QUICK FRUIT SALAD

green seedless grapes

cut-up cantaloupe

1 small can frozen limeade

Fill bowl with combination of grapes and cantaloupe. Thaw limeade and pour over all.

Easy and good!

Sara Margaret Johnson
via Susan Hill

VIRGINIA'S FRUIT SALAD

Serves 6

- ½ cup pecan halves, toasted
- 1 Tablespoon sherry vinegar
- 1 Tablespoon red wine vinegar
- 1 Tablespoon walnut oil
- 3 Tablespoons olive oil
- Salt and pepper, to taste
- 4 pears (about 1½ pounds total) halved, cored and diced
- 2 cups (12 ounces) green and red seedless grapes
- 2 green or red apples, halved, cored and diced

Spread pecans on a baking sheet and toast until lightly browned, in a 350° oven, 5 to 7 minutes.

Whisk vinegars and oils together in a small bowl and add salt and pepper to make a vinaigrette.

Combine the pears, grapes, apples and pecans in a salad bowl. Add the vinaigrette and toss to coat.

Virginia Farr

GRAPE SALAD

- 3-4 pounds red and green grapes
- 8 ounces cream cheese
- 8 ounces sour cream
- 1 Tablespoon vanilla
- ½ cup brown sugar
- ½ cup pecans or walnuts, chopped

Mix cream cheese, sour cream, vanilla and sugar in a bowl (best using a hand mixer set to medium). Fold in grapes and nuts. Refrigerate for at least 2 hours, then enjoy!

Del Harrington

BEVERLY'S AVOCADO AND GRAPEFRUIT SALAD

4-6 servings

4 ripe Hass avocados

2 large red grapefruits (or you can buy a jar of red grapefruit sections)

Brianna's Poppy Seed Dressing

butter lettuce or hydroponic lettuce

Arrange leaves of lettuce on salad plates. Cut avocados in half, remove the seed, and carefully peel off the skin. Cut each half into 4 thick slices. Use a large, sharp knife to slice the peel off the grapefruits (be sure to remove all the white pith), then cut the membranes to release the grapefruit segments. Alternate the grapefruit and avocado around the plate. Drizzle with poppy seed dressing.

Beverly Painter

MERRILL'S AVOCADO AND GRAPEFRUIT SALAD

This can be done two ways:

Peel and section a grapefruit and cut a ripe avocado into chunks. Mix with salad greens. Toss with an Italian dressing.

OR

Peel and section a grapefruit, place in a bowl and pour Italian salad dressing over grapefruit. Add salt. Slice ripe avocados in half, remove skin and place the half in a lettuce leaf. Using a slotted spoon, place grapefruit and dressing mixture inside each avocado letting it spill onto the lettuce leaf.

Plate and serve.

Merrill Tenney McKewen, aka MO

ERMA'S WALDORF SALAD

crisp red apples
celery
pecans
raisins
mayonnaise

Core and chop the apples and sprinkle with lemon juice to prevent browning. Add chopped celery and pecans, raisins and just enough mayonnaise to hold together. Serve chilled on a bed of fresh lettuce.

A perfect salad for any chicken entree. Easy, healthy, and delicious.

Mary Arrington Jones

FALL PEAR SALAD

salad greens (I like romaine hearts or red leaf)
4 pears, chunked or sliced
½ cup walnut hearts or pecans
1 small package of goat cheese
2 Tablespoons chopped chives
cracked black pepper

DRESSING
½ cup extra virgin olive oil
2 Tablespoons apple cider vinegar
2 Tablespoons orange juice
1 Tablespoon honey
Salt and pepper to taste

Whisk dressing ingredients in small bowl. Combine greens, pears and chives or arrange them on plates. Then put walnuts and cheese on each serving.

Susan Shands Jones

CRANBERRY RELISH

1 bag fresh cranberries

1 orange

1 lemon

1 apple

1 cup pecans or walnuts

1 small box strawberry Jell-o

¾ cup sugar

Cut lemon, orange and apple in half and remove seeds. Cut into smaller pieces and pulse in food processor. Process the cranberries and pecans or walnuts in the same way, removing each fruit to a mixing bowl as they are processed. Sprinkle with dry Jell-O powder and sugar; mix well. Refrigerate.

Serve with turkey and dressing and spinach madeleine, of course, and spread on a turkey sandwich the next day. Actually, it is an important component to "the perfect bite" which consists of a tiny amount of turkey, spinach madeleine, dressing, and cranberry all carefully placed on the fork...

👑 Anne Robertson from her family cookbook *First You Need a Big Pot*

FIVE-CUP FRUIT SALAD

1 cup pineapple chunks

1 cup mandarin orange sections

1 cup coconut

1 cup tiny marshmallows

1 cup sour cream

Mix together and refrigerate overnight.

👑 Mary Zimmerman

FROZEN FRUIT SALAD

Serves 15

- 1½ cups sour cream
- ¾ cup powdered sugar
- ⅛ teaspoon salt
- 2 Tablespoons lemon juice
- ½ cup sliced maraschino cherries
- 1 20-ounce can crushed pineapple, drained
- ¾ cup sliced seedless grapes
- 1 banana, diced (optional)
- ½ cup chopped pecans

Combine sour cream and sugar in large mixing bowl. Add salt and lemon juice, then remaining ingredients, blending evenly. Freeze in muffin tins with paper liners or 9 x 11-inch baking dish.

Kathryn McCraney from the Junior League of Jackson's *Southern Sideboards* cookbook

APPLE SAUCE AND RED HOT SALAD

FIRST AND THIRD LAYER:

- 1 box lemon Jell-O
- 1 cup boiling water
- ¾ cups red hots
- 1 cup apple sauce (you can use the healthy kind if it makes you feel better)

Melt red hots in boiling water. Dissolve Jell-O in red hot mixture and add apple sauce.

SECOND LAYER:

- 1 (8-ounce) package softened cream cheese (Mother's recipe calls for "Philly")
- ½ cup mayonnaise
- 1 cup chopped celery
- ½ cup chopped nuts
- powdered sugar

Sweeten cream cheese with powdered sugar to taste and mix all ingredients.

Pour ½ of first mixture in dish. Place in fridge until Jell-O sets. Then spread cream cheese mixture across Jell-O and let set up until slightly firm. Pour remaining Jell-O mixture on top to form third layer.

My mother used to make this pretty salad at Christmas. I usually make it in a 9x13 glass dish, but any clear glass dish of approximate size will do. Use a smaller container for thicker layers.

Kay Mortimer

PINEAPPLE LEMON SALAD

Serves 12

1 (20-ounce) can plus 1 (8-ounce) can crushed pineapple, reserving the juice

1 cup water

2 (3-ounce) boxes lemon Jell-O

1 (14-ounce) can sweetened condensed milk

1 cup mayonnaise

1 cup sharp cheddar cheese, grated

1 cup pecans, coarsely chopped

In a small saucepan, combine pineapple juice and water. Bring to a boil over medium-high heat. Add Jell-O, stirring to dissolve. Remove from heat and pour into a large bowl and let cool. Stir in condensed milk and mayonnaise, mixing slowly until smooth. Gently stir in pineapple, cheese (don't melt) and pecans. Spoon mixture into a 13 x 9-inch baking dish or wide, low serving bowl. Cover and refrigerate overnight until set. Garnish if desired.

Shirley Farrell

STRAWBERRY SALAD

2 boxes strawberry Jell-O

2 (8-ounce) packages frozen strawberries

1 large can crushed pineapple

3 bananas, sliced

1 cup pecans, chopped

1 small container sour cream

Mix Jell-O with 2 cups boiling water. Add partially thawed strawberries, then add pineapple, sliced bananas and pecans. Pour half of mixture in mold and refrigerate. Let set, then spread sour cream on top of this layer. Pour remaining Jell-O and fruit mixture on top of sour cream. Return to refrigerator and chill until set.

Miriam Weems via her sister-in-law, Betty Weems Clarkson. Submitted in Miriam's memory by Tommy Weems.

HEAVENLY SALAD

1 box lemon gelatin

1 box orange gelatin

1 cup boiling water

1 small can crushed pineapple

3 small cans mandarin oranges

1 large package miniature marshmallows, optional

Combine boxes of gelatin. Add 1 cup boiling water. Add undrained pineapple and oranges. Stir in marshmallows. Pour into 9 x 13 Pyrex dish. Refrigerate.

TOPPING

2 Tablespoons all-purpose flour

½ cup sugar

1 egg, beaten

½ cup pineapple juice

1 (8-ounce) package cream cheese, softened

Combine flour and sugar in a small saucepan. Add egg and pineapple juice, mixing well. Bring to a boil over low heat, stirring constantly. Cook and stir until smooth and thickened. Remove from heat; add cream cheese and beat until smooth. Cool before spreading over gelatin mixture.

 Lucy Clark

FROSTED LIME SALAD

1 (3-ounce) package lime gelatin

1 cup boiling water

1 (20-ounce) can crushed pineapple

½ cup celery, finely chopped

1 cup chopped pecans

1 cup small curd cottage cheese

1 Tablespoon chopped pimento (optional...I don't add)

1 (3-ounce) package cream cheese

1 Tablespoon mayonnaise

1 teaspoon lemon juice

Dissolve gelatin in boiling water. Cool until syrupy. Stir in pineapple, pecans, cottage cheese, celery and pimento. Turn into large salad mold, loaf pan, or Pyrex pan rinsed in cold water. Chill. When firm, unmold or leave in pan. Blend cream cheese, mayonnaise, and lemon juice, beating until smooth, and frost top of salad.

I use the frosted lime salad a lot. It's a little sweet and can almost serve as a dessert on a large buffet.

Walterine Odom

ORANGE SALAD MOLD

Serves 8

  2 small cans mandarin oranges

  1 large can crushed pineapple

  2 small packages orange gelatin

  1 (6-ounce) can frozen orange juice

Drain oranges and pineapple, saving juices. Add enough water to juices to make 3½ cups liquid. Heat 2 cups of this liquid and dissolve the gelatin in it. Add remaining liquid. Chill until slightly thickened; add fruit and undiluted orange juice. Chill until firm.

Virginia Ezelle

GREEN STUFF

  1 package lime Jell-O (I use sugar-free)

  1 small package Philadelphia cream cheese

  1 small can crushed pineapple, drained

  ½ pint whipping cream, unwhipped

Dissolve Jell-O in 1 cup hot water. Add cream cheese with a wire whisk. Add other ingredients, stir and chill for several hours in an 8-inch mold.

One of my husband's family favorites. I avoided trying it for years but when I did, I was pleasantly surprised!

Dorothy Hawkins

SEBELLE SALAD

1 package lime Jell-O

1 package lemon Jell-O

2 cups hot water

Mix and stir well; let stand until other ingredients are mixed.

1 can Dime Brand sweetened condensed milk

1 (8-ounce) package cream cheese, softened

1 large can crushed pineapple

¼ cup mayonnaise

1 cup chopped pecans or walnuts

Gently mix all ingredients. Pour concoction into a Pyrex pan and refrigerate overnight. To serve, cut into squares. Line a platter or plates with pretty lettuce and, if desired, add a dollop of mayonnaise on top.

It sounds gross, but it's really wonderful. It is a part of the traditional Bourdeaux Thanksgiving and Christmas dinners.

Ellen Bourdeaux

MY SISTER'S PRETZEL SALAD

Serves 15-20

CRUST

2 cups crushed pretzels

¾ cup melted margarine

3 Tablespoons powdered sugar

Mix and refrigerate for 30 minutes. Then press into a 9 x 13 Pyrex pan. Cook in a preheated 400° oven for 8 minutes and cool.

CREAM CHEESE LAYER

8 ounces cream cheese

1 cup sugar

8 ounces Cool Whip

Mix, pour over crust and refrigerate 2 hours.

TOPPING

6 ounces strawberry Jell-O

2 cups boiling water

2 (10-ounce) cartons frozen strawberries

Dissolve Jell-O in the boiling water; add frozen strawberries and stir until strawberries thaw.

Pour over cream cheese layer and refrigerate until set. Will keep for days in the refrigerator.

Chyrl Grubbs

Pasta

Bruschetta Couscous Salad	32	Mary's Pasta Salad	22
Chyrl's Quick Dinner Salad	29	Orzo Salad	32
Claire's Pasta Salad	23	Pasta and Asparagus	21
Cobb Pasta Salad	31	Pasta Salad with Chicken	26
Cold Pasta Salad	24	Roasted Shrimp and Orzo Pasta Salad	33
Couscous Carnivale	19	Sesame Noodles	20
Faye's Pasta Salad	29	Sesame Pasta Salad	20
Greek Pasta Salad	28	St. James' Pasta Salad	25
Grilled Chicken Pasta Salad	27	Summer Orzo Salad	33
Ivy's Pasta Salad	23	Summer Pasta Salad	30
Kathryn's Pasta Salad with Vermicelli	22	Thai Noodle Salad	21
Kathryn's Penne Pasta Salad	24	Three Pepper Pasta Salad	28
Lemon Caper Pasta Salad	25		

COUSCOUS CARNIVALE

Serves 8-10

- 1½ cups whole-wheat couscous
- ½ teaspoon salt
- 1½ cups water
- 1 mango, peeled and finely diced
- 1 Granny Smith apple, skin on, cored and finely diced
- 1 red pepper, finely diced
- 1 yellow pepper, finely diced
- 4 green onions or scallions, sliced thinly on the diagonal
- ½ cup dried cranberries or dried cherries
- ½ cup sliced almonds
- ¼ cup chopped flat leaf parsley

DRESSING

- ½ cup extra virgin olive oil
- ½ cup cider vinegar
- 1 teaspoon salt
- ½ teaspoon pepper

Place couscous and salt in heat-proof bowl. Boil water and pour over couscous. Cover bowl with plastic wrap and let sit for 5 minutes or until the liquid is absorbed. Remove plastic wrap, fluff couscous with a fork, and allow it to cool completely.

Combine all the remaining salad ingredients in a large mixing bowl. Add the cooled couscous and toss to combine. Mix in dressing and toss thoroughly.

This can be served at room temperature or cold. Saves well, too, if you have any left. People love this dish!

Mary Nichols

SESAME NOODLES

1 pound thin spaghetti, linguine or fettucini

¼ cup sesame oil

3 Tablespoons soy sauce or Tamari

¼ teaspoon black pepper

½ sweet red pepper, finely diced

¼ cup watercress leaves, chopped

½ teaspoon chopped garlic

Boil pasta in salted water al dente, drain and submerge in ice water for 30 seconds. Drain off cold water and dry off as much as possible. Add soy, sesame oil and black pepper immediately and mix to coat. Add red pepper, watercress and garlic. Mix thoroughly. Refrigerate overnight. Serve cold.

Louisa Dixon

SESAME PASTA SALAD

3 Tablespoons soy sauce

2 Tablespoon rice wine vinegar

½ teaspoon dried red pepper flakes

2 Tablespoon firmly packed brown sugar

½ cup creamy peanut butter

1 Tablespoon sesame oil

1 teaspoon ground ginger

½ to 1 cup chicken broth

½ cup chopped green onion

fresh asparagus, blanched and cut in small pieces, optional

1 pound angel hair pasta, cooked, rinsed and drained

Combine all ingredients except pasta, onions and asparagus in saucepan and simmer, stirring, until thickened and smooth. Takes a while. Cool slightly. Toss pasta with sauce, adding green onion and asparagus, if desired. Serve at room temperature.

Julie Moore

THAI NOODLE SALAD

Serves 4

1 (8-ounce) package vermicelli

2 carrots, grated

1 cucumber, peeled or "forked" down the sides, thinly sliced (you can seed if you fear indigestion)

¼ cup (or more) coarsely chopped fresh mint

dry roasted peanuts, coarsely chopped

CILANTRO DRESSING

½ cup (or more) cilantro, chopped

1 jalapeno, roughly chopped (remove seeds if you don't want heat, leave them in if you do)

¼ cup fresh lime juice

1 Tablespoon fish sauce (or can use soy sauce)

1 Tablespoon honey

1½ teaspoon sesame oil

¼ teaspoon salt

Place dressing ingredients in food processor and process until smooth. Scrape down sides.

Cook pasta according to package directions. Drain, rinse, and place in bowl; set aside.

Toss together the pasta, cilantro dressing, carrots, cucumber mint and peanuts. Sprinkle with more chopped peanuts.

👑 Margaret Tohill

PASTA AND ASPARAGUS

⅔ cup olive oil

¼ cup fresh lemon juice

2 teaspoons seasoned salt

1 teaspoon onion, grated

1 small clove garlic, crushed

1 bunch asparagus (10 stalks cooked al dente, cut in thirds; don't use woody ends)

1 pound angel hair pasta, cooked al dente; rinse and drain well after cooking

½ package fresh dill, chopped

Combine all the ingredients except pasta, asparagus and dill. To serve, toss pasta with marinade. Add dill and asparagus, toss again. Serve at room temperature.

👑 Julie Moore

KATHRYN'S PASTA SALAD with VERMICELLI

Serves 12

- 12 ounces vermicelli, cooked
- ½ red onion, chopped
- ½ green pepper, chopped
- 1 can sliced black olives
- 1 (8-ounce) bottle Wishbone Italian Dressing
- 1 package dry Good Seasons Zesty Italian Dressing
- ½ jar McCormick Salad Supreme
- 2 tomatoes, chopped

Mix and refrigerate. Make 24 hours ahead.

Kathryn McCraney

MARY'S PASTA SALAD

- 1 package spaghetti
- tomato
- green onions
- cucumber
- mayonnaise
- Italian salad dressing
- garlic salt
- 1 teaspoon mustard
- pinch of sugar
- Parmesan cheese

Cook spaghetti and cool. Add to chopped onion, tomato and cucumbers. Add Italian dressing, then mayonnaise and lots of garlic salt. Add remaining ingredients. Mix well. Chill overnight. Toss before serving.

Mary Zimmerman

CLAIRE'S PASTA SALAD

1 (12-ounce) package vermicelli, cooked and cooled

1 red bell pepper, chopped

4 green onions, chopped

1 small can sliced black olives

DRESSING

½ cup olive oil

3 Tablespoons lemon juice

3 Tablespoons mayonnaise

2 Tablespoons Cavender's Greek Seasoning

Combine pasta, pepper, onion and olives in mixing bowl. Whisk dressing, blending well. Toss everything!

👑 Claire Barksdale

IVY'S PASTA SALAD

Serves 10-12

1-pound package penne pasta, cooked, drained and rinsed with cold water

1 cup pitted Greek olives, sliced

1 can hearts of palm, drained, rinsed, thickly sliced

2 cucumbers, seeded, coarsely chopped

2 tomatoes, coarsely chopped

1 cup goat cheese, crumbled

DRESSING

2 cups Greek yogurt

¼ cup olive oil

1 Tablespoon fresh dill or 1 teaspoon dried dill

1 Tablespoon lemon juice

2 cloves garlic, minced

salt and pepper

Whisk dressing in bowl and set aside. Combine pasta and vegetables and toss with dressing. Add goat cheese. Chill.

👑 Ivy Alley

KATHRYN'S PENNE PASTA SALAD

½ cup olive oil

¼ cup balsamic vinegar

4 Tablespoons sugar

2 Tablespoons country Dijon mustard

3 cloves garlic, minced

1 pound penne pasta, boiled

Parmesan

fresh basil

grape tomatoes

pine nuts

Mix all together.

Kathryn McCraney

COLD PASTA SALAD

1 box bow-tie pasta

chicken broth

1 jar marinated artichoke hearts (using about ⅓ of juice)

1 small can black olives, sliced

1½ cup cherry or grape tomatoes, cut in half

4 Tablespoons Cavender's Greek Seasoning

1 cup mayonnaise, or more if you like

1 green bell pepper, diced

¾ cup roast red bell peppers

1 cup asparagus, blanched and cut into 1-inch pieces

2 cups yellow squash and zucchini, sliced and cut into halves

Cook pasta in chicken broth. Combine remaining ingredients and add to hot, drained pasta. Toss all together and refrigerate before seasoning.

Del Harrington

ST. JAMES' PASTA SALAD

1 pound pasta (vermicelli, bow-tie, whatever), cooked and cooled

½ red onion, chopped

½ bell pepper, chopped

1 tall can pitted black olives

1 or 2 cans artichoke hearts, sliced

Toss the above together and add:

1 package dry Italian salad dressing

½ bottle Salad Supreme

About ½ regular-size bottle of olive oil Italian dressing—more or less

Chill and serve.

👑 Jan Wofford

LEMON-CAPER PASTA SALAD

Serves 10

1 box bow-tie pasta

1 cup lemon juice

1 jar nonpareil capers (8-10 ounces)

⅓ cup lemon pepper seasoning

1½ Tablespoon Tony Chachere's seasoning

1 cup celery, chopped

⅓ cup green onions, chopped

2 cups mayonnaise

2 cups diced fresh tomatoes, cut into medium size pieces

Cook bow-tie pasta according to directions. Mix first 4 ingredients until blended in large bowl. Add remaining ingredients and stir. Shrimp, chicken or salmon can be added for a main course salad.

Buddie Barksdale via her sister,
Melanie Williams

PASTA SALAD *with* CHICKEN

Serves 20-30

- 1-1½ pounds linguine or penne, cooked according to package directions
- ½ cup pine nuts
- ½ cup chicken stock
- 6 chicken breast halves, baked or boiled, cut into bite-size pieces (If you use 1½ pounds pasta, add 2 chicken breast halves.)
- 1 (15-ounce) can garbanzo beans, rinsed and drained
- 2 cans artichoke hearts, chopped
- 1 package frozen shelled edamame, thawed,
- ½ pound fresh mushrooms, sliced
- 1 (20-ounce) jar stuffed olives, drained and sliced
- 1 (20-ounce) can pitted black olives, drained and left whole
- 1 red bell pepper, seeded and diced

CURRY DIJON DRESSING

- ½ cup olive oil
- ½ cup canola oil
- 3 Tablespoons red wine vinegar
- ¼ cup chopped parsley
- 1 Tablespoon Dijon mustard
- 1 teaspoon curry powder

Mix salad ingredients and toss with dressing. (1 cup Vivienne's Romano Cheese Dressing can be substituted for the dressing—you still need to add the curry powder. Order it by calling 1-800-827-0778.)

Julie Moore via Pat Cothern

GRILLED CHICKEN PASTA SALAD

1 bag baby spinach

½ cup sun-dried tomatoes, chopped

½ cup feta cheese, crumbled

1 bag bow-tie pasta, cooked and cooled

4-5 grilled chicken breasts, chopped and cooled

BALSAMIC VINAIGRETTE

2 Tablespoons rice wine vinegar

2 teaspoons Dijon mustard

4 dashes Tabasco

5 teaspoons sugar

1 teaspoon dried oregano

6 Tablespoons balsamic vinegar

5 gloves garlic, peeled and minced

1 teaspoon black pepper

1 teaspoon Worcestershire sauce

1½ teaspoon salt

1 cup olive oil

Put all dressing ingredients except oil in a food processor or blender. Process for about 20 seconds. Slowly add in oil with machine running. Store in fridge. Best made a least a day ahead.

Combine spinach, sun-dried tomatoes, feta cheese, pasta and chicken. Toss everything with about half of the dressing and add more as needed.

The best part of the salad is that everything can be made ahead of time and tossed together at the last minute. It is also great leftover. I have used the pre-grilled breasts sold in the bag. You can add whatever you like.

Lisa Ireland

GREEK PASTA SALAD

1 (12-ounce) package pasta of your choice, cooked according to package directions

1 bunch chopped green onions, tops included

1 small can sliced ripe olives

Add anything else you would like—Parmesan cheese, chicken, shrimp, green or yellow pepper, etc.

DRESSING

4 Tablespoons mayonnaise

4 Tablespoons lemon juice

¾ cup olive oil

4 Tablespoons Cavender's Greek Seasoning (I use 2½-3 Tablespoons)

Mix dressing, add to pasta and other ingredients, and mix well. Serve cold.

Sara Margaret Johnson

THREE PEPPER PASTA SALAD

Leftover skinless, boneless chicken breast (I marinate mine in salt, pepper, lemon juice and olive oil and grill)

3 bell peppers—one each of green, red and yellow

1 bunch spring onions

2 boxes bow-tie pasta (I use one box white and one wheat)

1 package sun dried tomatoes

salt and pepper to taste

good balsamic vinegar

extra virgin olive oil

Adjust the amounts according to how much chicken you have. I usually use about 6 or 8 breasts for the ingredients listed above.

Chop the vegetables and chicken, add to hot cooked pasta. Season liberally with salt, pepper, oil and vinegar and toss. Adjust seasonings as needed, tossing lightly so the salad will not get sticky. Serve at room temperature or chilled.

This is my family's favorite summer-time pasta salad. I made it up with the ingredients I had on hand and they all adored it. It is plain enough for the young picky ones, heart-healthy and low-fat for the older ones, and delicious to all.

Mary Arrington Jones

FAYE'S PASTA SALAD

Serves 12-16

1 bunch of green onions, chopped

1 large jar of ripe olives, sliced

1 large jar diced pimento

4½ Tablespoons Cavender's Greek Seasoning

¾ cup mayonnaise

¾ cup extra virgin olive oil

4½ Tablespoons fresh lemon juice (I use more)

1 box angel hair spaghetti

Combine first 5 ingredients. Set aside. Measure and set aside olive oil and lemon juice, separately. Cook pasta until desired doneness. Combine with mayonnaise mixture. Add olive oil and lemon juice. Mix well.

Can be served warm or cold. Goodies settle to the bottom. Shrimp, chicken or ham can be added for a main dish.

Lynda Wright

CHYRL'S QUICK DINNER SALAD

1 box Pasta Roni-Caesar, cooked as directed on box

Substitute for dressing
½ cup mayonnaise

1 seasoning packet from Pasta Roni

½ cup milk

For meat use one of the following:
1 deli rotisserie chicken, deboned and shredded

1 pound shrimp, peeled, deveined and cooked

1 pound crab meat, drained

1 pound sausage, cooked and drained

Mix drained pasta, dressing and meat. If more liquid is needed just mix another ½ cup of mayonnaise and ½ cup of milk.

Chyrl Grubbs

SUMMER PASTA SALAD

Serves 12-16

16-ounce box of bow-tie, or any bite-sized pasta

2 pounds total of meats and/or veggies

VEGETABLE SUGGESTIONS:

cooked or grilled asparagus, bell pepper, broccoli, carrots, eggplant, green beans, mushrooms, squash, zucchini

fresh uncooked avocado, celery, cherry tomatoes, cucumber.

canned artichoke hearts, beans, drained and rinsed

MEAT SUGGESTIONS:

chicken breast, crabmeat, ham, Italian sausage, lobster, shrimp, tuna

EXTRA FLAVOR SUGGESTIONS:

3 green onions, small red onion

2 cups cheese and goodies from a mix of the following: crumbled feta or goat cheese, shaved Parmesan, chopped olives, roasted cashews, sun-dried tomatoes; capers, pine nuts, sunflower seeds

3 Tablespoons fresh herb selections: basil, cilantro, dill, parsley, rosemary, tarragon

2 teaspoons orange or lemon zest

Cook pasta in 1 gallon boiling water with 2 Tablespoons salt until just tender. Drain but DO NOT rinse. Spread pasta on cookie sheet to cool and dry.

Prepare vegetable and meat selections. Mix extra flavor suggestions with vegetables and meats.

Add pasta and mix together well. Refrigerate salad or serve room temperature.

Add dressing and mix well 15 minutes before serving.

CREAMY VINAIGRETTE DRESSING

¼ cup rice wine vinegar or lemon juice

2 Tablespoons Dijon mustard or mayonnaise

1 large clove garlic, minced

Pinch of salt and freshly-ground pepper

⅔ cup olive oil

In a 2-cup measuring cup, stir vinegar (or lemon juice) and mustard (or mayonnaise) together. Whisk in garlic, salt, and pepper. Measure oil into another cup. Slowly whisk oil into mixture to make an emulsified vinaigrette.

Great one-dish meal with fresh summer veggies, meat or not.

Jeanne Luckett, adapted from "USA Weekend" in *The Clarion-Ledger*

COBB PASTA SALAD

Serves 8-10

1 pound wagon-wheel pasta—I use a smaller, thinner pasta like spaghettini

2 cups cooked chicken, cut up

10 ounces bacon, fried and crumbled or a whole container Oscar Mayer Real Bacon Pieces

4-5 cups fresh spinach, sliced thinly

1 cup black olives, sliced

4 ounces Bleu cheese, crumbled

2 huge ripe Mississippi tomatoes or 6-8 Roma tomatoes, diced

5-6 green onions, sliced

purple cabbage, shredded, optional

artichoke hearts, cut up, optional

water chestnuts, optional

HONEY DIJON DRESSING

1- 2 Tablespoons Dijon mustard

½ cup some sort of good wine vinegar, without too much of a whang to it—balsamic is good

½ cup extra virgin olive oil

coarse-ground pepper

3 great big cloves of garlic, pressed

1 teaspoon honey or sugar-honey is better since it doesn't have to dissolve

Mix dressing well and let sit at least 15 minutes—the longer the better.

For the chicken, I use 4 large frozen skinless boneless breasts and boil gently no longer than 25-30 minutes so they won't get tough and dry. Add some water to the chicken broth and boil the pasta to the al dente stage, not too soft or gooey—start at 12 minutes, taste a piece, boil a few more minutes if need be; some pasta takes up to 20 minutes if the pieces are thick. Rinse pasta with cold water for a few minutes and let it sit there; could even dribble a little olive oil or some of the dressing over it so it won't stick together, especially if you put it in the fridge.

Combine all other salad ingredients and stir them up. Add the pasta and mix it well with other ingredients. Add dressing gradually, mixing well. I think this is about the right amount of dressing, but I hate too-dressing-y salad, so don't put so much that it pools at the bottom of the bowl, but just coats all the ingredients. You can eat this immediately or stick it in the fridge for a while.

Margaret Tohill

BRUCHETTA COUSCOUS SALAD

Serves 10

16 ounces couscous

½ small red onion, finely chopped

3 cloves garlic, minced

3 ribs celery, finely chopped

20 ounces cherry tomatoes, quartered

½ cup Parmesan cheese, grated

1 cup small fresh mozzarella balls, quartered

½ cup fresh basil leaves

¼ cup extra virgin olive oil

2 Tablespoons balsamic vinegar

salt and pepper

Cook couscous according to directions. Allow to cool. In large bowl combine couscous with onion, garlic, celery, basil, Parmesan cheese, tomatoes, mozzarella, olive oil and vinegar. Stir to combine and add salt and pepper. Can serve immediately, but flavors improve if allowed to sit 30 minutes.

Durden Moss from *The Clarion-Ledger*

ORZO SALAD

½ cup lemon juice

½ cup olive oil

2 Tablespoons chopped fresh oregano

2 Tablespoons chopped fresh chives

½ teaspoon salt

½ teaspoon ground black pepper

1 box orzo pasta, cooked and drained

1 cucumber, diced

1 pint grape tomatoes, halved

1 jar quartered artichoke hearts, drained

1 jar whole pitted olives, drained

3½ ounces feta cheese, crumbled

In a small bowl, combine lemon juice, olive oil, oregano, chives, salt and pepper. In a large bowl, combine orzo, cucumber, tomatoes, artichoke hearts, olives and feta cheese. Pour lemon juice mixture over the pasta mixture, stirring to combine.

Laura Morgan

SUMMER ORZO SALAD

1 package orzo pasta, cooked and drained well

1 package crumbled feta cheese

¾ to 1 cup chopped dried cranberries and/or chopped dried cherries

¾ cup chopped, toasted walnuts or pecans

1½ cups roughly chopped baby arugula (basil, if you choose)

juice of ½ lemon

salt and pepper

Toss orzo with olive oil to coat, set aside. Add remaining ingredients and toss together.

Mary Nichols

ROASTED SHRIMP AND ORZO PASTA SALAD

1½ pound medium shrimp

1 pound package of orzo pasta, cooked, rinsed and tossed with olive oil to coat

1 (3.25-ounce) bottle of capers, drained

juice of 4-5 large lemons

⅓ tube of anchovy paste (located in the canned fish section of grocery)

½ red and yellow bell peppers, diced

4-5 green onions, sliced

3 stalks celery, diced

¼ cup chopped parsley

Cavender's Greek Seasoning to taste (I use the blue can...no salt)

salt and pepper

Heat oven to 425°. Peel and devein shrimp if necessary. Toss shrimp in olive oil and season with salt and pepper. Place on a baking sheet and roast for 2-3 minutes, turn and roast another 2 minutes.

Toss shrimp with all ingredients and marinate for 6 hours or overnight before serving.

Claire Barksdale

Chicken, Beef & Seafood

Al's Favorite Chicken Salad	42
Chinese Chicken Salad with Cilantro Sesame Dressing	41
Chutney Chicken Salad	45
Classic Seafood Louis	47
Congealed Chicken Salad	42
County Down Curried Shrimp Salad	50
Crab Salad with Asparagus, Avocado and Lime	48
Curried Cranberry Chicken Salad	43
Curried Chicken Salad	44
Deviled Eggs	46
Dorothy's Chicken Salad	39
Egg Salad	46
Fabulous Chicken Salad	45
Fried Green Tomato and Grilled Shrimp with Black-eyed Pea and Corn Salsa	49
Grilled Steak Salad	47
Kakow's Curried Tuna Salad	51
Lime Shrimp	50
Mary's Meeting Salad	38
Mediterranean Chicken Salad	38
My Mediterranean Diet-Inspired Salad	39
Oriental Chicken Salad	40
Seared Tuna Salad	52
Smoked Chicken Salad	44
Virgie's Tuna Salad	51
Vogue Overnight Salad	37
White Bean and Tuna Salad	53

VOGUE OVERNIGHT SALAD

½ large honeydew melon, peeled and cut into pieces

6 chicken breast halves, skinned and boned

1 cup white wine

1 cup water

1 teaspoon black peppercorns

celery tops from 2 stalks celery

4 Tablespoons parsley, chopped

2 stalks celery, finely chopped (don't use processor)

LEMON-GINGER DRESSING

⅔ cup Hellman's mayonnaise

⅔ cup sour cream

rind of one small lemon, grated

4 Tablespoons lemon juice

2 teaspoons honey

3 inches ginger root, peeled and grated

salt

pepper

Blend dressing ingredients. Cover and refrigerate. Cut honeydew, place in separate bowl and refrigerate.

Bring wine, water, peppercorns and celery tops to a gentle boil; add chicken, cover and poach until done. Remove chicken from stock and cut into bite-sized pieces (not too small). Place in bowl with the parsley and celery; cover and refrigerate.

Just before serving, pour off any juice the melon has exuded and gently toss chicken mixture, cut melon and dressing. Serve on a bed of Bibb, also known as butterhead or Boston, lettuce.

Everything can be done the day before. Just be sure to store chicken, melon and dressing in separate containers. Do not combine until ready to serve.

♔ Julie Moore

MEDITERRANEAN CHICKEN SALAD

3 pounds chicken breasts, baked and meat
   pulled off in large bite-size pieces

½ cup olive oil

1½ teaspoon dried oregano

¼ pound green beans, cooked

juice of 1 lemon

¾ cup black olives, sliced

2 Tablespoons capers, drained

8 cherry tomatoes, halved

Cover and marinate the cooked chicken in the olive
oil and oregano for at least 1 hour.

Toss with the remaining ingredients and add salt
and pepper to taste.

Louisa Dixon

MARY'S MEETING SALAD

Serves 8

4 cups cubed, cooked chicken breast

1 (16-ounce) can black beans, drained

¾ red onion, chopped

½ red bell pepper, chopped

½ yellow bell pepper, chopped

¼ cup chopped fresh cilantro

½ cup sour cream

¼ cup mayonnaise

½ teaspoon garlic powder

1 jalapeno pepper, finely chopped

1 teaspoon lime juice

1 teaspoon salt

½ teaspoon pepper

½ cup toasted pine nuts

Combine chicken, beans, onion, peppers and cilantro in a large bowl.

In a small bowl whisk sour cream and mayonnaise together. Stir in garlic powder, jalapeno pepper
and lime juice. Add to chicken mixture. Add salt and
pepper, toss.

Refrigerate at least one hour before serving. Just
before serving toss in pine nuts. Serve on a bed of
lettuce or spread on bagels.

Angelyn Cannada

DOROTHY'S CHICKEN SALAD

3 whole chicken breasts

1 medium onion

2 carrots

1 leek

1 teaspoon thyme

1 bay leaf

6 parsley sprigs

12 black peppercorns

4 cloves

⅓ cup olive oil

1½ teaspoons dried oregano

2 Tablespoons capers

8 cherry tomatoes

juice of one lemon

¼ pound green beans, cooked

¾ can black olives

Salt and pepper

Cook chicken breasts in water to cover with onion, carrots, leek, thyme, bay leaf, parsley, peppercorns, cloves and salt. De-bone chicken, chop, and combine in a bowl with olive oil and oregano. Add capers, tomatoes, lemon juice, green beans, black olives, salt and pepper.

👑 Anne Robertson via Dorothy Howorth. This recipe is in Anne's family cookbook, *First You Need a Big Pot*

MY MEDITERRANEAN DIET-INSPIRED SALAD

Use whatever amounts you wish of the following ingredients:

chicken tenders

fresh mushrooms, sliced

fresh spinach, washed

green onion, chopped

avocado, sliced

Cut chicken tenders to bite size and sauté in olive oil. Season with salt, pepper, and ground coriander seed. Drain on paper towels.

In olive oil, sauté mushrooms seasoned with salt and pepper.

Put fresh spinach in a large bowl, add chopped green onions, sliced avocado, the chicken and mushrooms.

Toss with dressing and add salt and freshly-ground black pepper on top.

DRESSING

5 scant Tablespoons white balsamic vinegar

½ teaspoon salt

½ teaspoon white pepper

½ teaspoon sugar

½ cup olive oil

Several crushed garlic cloves

👑 Betty Allin

ORIENTAL CHICKEN SALAD

2 heads of lettuce (red leaf, romaine, iceberg, Bibb), washed and torn

4 chicken breast filets

8 green onions

2 small bags sliced almonds, lightly toasted

3 packages wontons, sliced into strips and fried in peanut oil

¼ cup sesame seeds

¼ cup fresh cilantro, chopped

DRESSING

4 Tablespoons sugar

2 teaspoons salt

4 Tablespoons sesame oil (located in the oriental food section at the grocery)

6 Tablespoons salad oil

6 Tablespoons red wine vinegar

2½ Tablespoons black pepper

Chicken may either be grilled (season with Tony Chachere's) or lightly breaded in flour and then sautéed in olive oil. Slice chicken, after it has cooled, into thin strips.

Heat about 2 inches of peanut oil in a skillet and lightly brown wonton strips. Drain on paper towels to remove excess oil. Store in airtight container.

Toast almonds in a single layer at 300° until lightly browned (about 5-7 minutes).

Mix all ingredients in a large bowl and toss.

Mix dressing ingredients. Prior to serving salad, shake dressing very well. Pour small amounts over salad, toss, and then add a bit more dressing, if needed. The dressing coats very well, so you may only use half of the dressing recipe for two heads of lettuce.

Claire Barksdale

CHINESE CHICKEN SALAD *with* CILANTRO SESAME DRESSING

1 teaspoon butter

5 Tablespoons toasted sesame seeds, divided

2/3 cup slivered almonds

1/4 cup brown sugar

1 head lettuce

1½ cups chow mein noodles

3 carrots, grated

Sesame Fried Chicken *(see recipe below)*

CILANTRO SESAME DRESSING

1 cup mayonnaise

1 cup cilantro leaves

3 Tablespoons rice wine vinegar

2 teaspoons sesame oil

1 teaspoon sugar

1 teaspoon fresh ginger, minced

pinch of cayenne

Put all dressing ingredients in a food processor and blend until smooth. Store in the fridge.

Melt butter in skillet, add 2 tablespoons sesame seeds, almonds and brown sugar. Sauté for about 2 minutes, then spread on foil to cool.

Toss dressing with lettuce, chow mein noodles, carrots, sesame/almond mixture and cooked chicken.

SESAME FRIED CHICKEN

4 boneless chicken breasts,
    cut into 1-inch chunks

1 cup buttermilk

3/4 cup flour

1/4 cup cornstarch

2 teaspoons paprika

2 teaspoons salt

oil for frying chicken

Make Sesame Fried Chicken—marinate chicken in buttermilk for about 1 hour. Whisk together flour, corn starch, 3 tablespoons sesame seeds, paprika and salt. Drain chicken and toss in flour mixture. Cook in hot oil until done (about 3-5 minutes per batch).

You can use any kind of chicken but Sesame Fried Chicken is the best.

Lisa Ireland

CONGEALED CHICKEN SALAD

Serves 16-20

- 5-6 pound hen boiled with celery, onion and salt until tender. Cool, de-bone and cut up.
- 2 cups celery, chopped
- 3 hard-boiled eggs, chopped
- 1 cup small English peas, drained
- 1 envelope of gelatin
- 1 cup boiling chicken stock
- 1 Tablespoon India relish
- 1 Tablespoon Worcestershire sauce
- 2 cups mayonnaise
- Pinch of salt

Mix first 4 ingredients. Soften gelatin in ¼ cup cold water, then dissolve in the hot chicken stock; add relish, Worcestershire and salt, then stir into chicken mixture. When cool, add mayonnaise. Refrigerate until serving time.

This recipe is from my Aunt Cordelia, from Live Oak, Florida.

Laura Damon Wofford

AL'S FAVORITE CHICKEN SALAD

- Breast meat from roasted chicken
- 2 stalks celery
- ¾ cup toasted walnuts or pecans, chopped
- 3 Tablespoons orange marmalade
- Dukes or homemade mayonnaise
- lemon juice to taste, at least ½ lemon
- salt and pepper

Chop first 3 ingredients—add to other ingredients. Enjoy!

Margaret Barrett Simon

CURRIED CHICKEN SALAD

4 cans premium chicken breast (I like the brand at Sam's the best, but Tyson is okay, too)

1 (16-ounce) jar artichoke relish (I like Low Country Produce), or two 8-ounce jars of Braswell's

1 cup Hellman's mayonnaise

1 cup golden raisins or other dried fruit

1 to 1½ cups nuts (pecans, peanuts, cashews or mixed)

2 Tablespoons curry powder

Drain and shred the chicken breast (I use my hands). Add artichoke relish and mix. Start with 1 cup of Hellman's. You may add more to taste. Stir in the raisins and nuts. Adjust mayonnaise to desired consistency. Stir in curry powder. I use a mixture of regular and Madras, which is hotter. Feel free to change up the dried fruit (apricots, cranberries, cherries) and nuts, depending on what you have on hand. And if you like cooking your own chicken, that's great, too—just shred instead of chop it. If I cook my own chicken, I boil it with one whole onion studded with cloves, one cinnamon stick and a bay leaf. That takes the "boiled chicken smell" out of your kitchen and lightly infuses the chicken with a subtle flavor.

This is best made a few hours to a day ahead. I wouldn't stuff tomatoes with it, but it's wonderful with fruit, on a sandwich or by itself. Artichoke relish is seasonal—it's made with Jerusalem artichokes. Braswell's has gotten hard to find locally, so I have been ordering from Low Country Produce online. Stock up when you find it!

👑 Jane Alexander

CURRIED CRANBERRY CHICKEN SALAD

Serves 4

- 2 cups cooked chicken breasts, chopped
- 1 medium apple (a good one like Granny Smith or Fuji) cut into ½-inch pieces
- ¾ cup dried cranberries
- ½ cup thinly-sliced celery
- ½ cup chopped walnuts
- 2 Tablespoons chopped green onions (I use more)
- ¾ cup mayonnaise
- Juice of a fresh lime (might need more)
- 1½ teaspoons really good curry powder

Combine first 6 ingredients in a large bowl. Combine mayonnaise, lime juice and curry powder; add to chicken mixture, stirring well. Chill thoroughly.

Margaret Tohill

SMOKED CHICKEN SALAD

- 1 whole smoked chicken
- 2 Tablespoons chives, chopped
- ¼ cup parsley, chopped
- salt and pepper to taste
- ½ cup mayonnaise
- 1 teaspoon garlic powder
- 1 teaspoon lemon juice

Grind dark meat and chop white meat of chicken. Mix all ingredients with a fork or spoon. Add extra mayonnaise as needed.

Del Harrington

FABULOUS CHICKEN SALAD

4 cups cooked chicken breast, cubed

¾ pounds green grapes, cut in half

1 can water chestnuts, sliced

1½ cups chopped pecans

1½ cups chopped celery

DRESSING

2 cups mayonnaise

4 Tablespoons red wine vinegar

3 Tablespoons soy sauce

½ cup minced onion

4 teaspoons curry powder

2 teaspoons ground ginger

Mix dressing separately and let stand one hour. Mix chicken, grapes, water chestnuts, pecans and celery, then combine with dressing and chill one hour before serving.

 Rebecca Wiggs

CHUTNEY CHICKEN SALAD

Serves 6

1 cup mayonnaise

½ cup Major Grey Chutney

8 chicken breast halves, cooked, cut in bite size pieces

2 stalks celery, coarsely chopped

4 green onions, coarsely chopped

1 Granny Smith apple, unpeeled, coarsely chopped, sprinkled with lemon juice

½ cup red seedless grapes, sliced

½ cup chopped pecans, toasted

2 cups cooked brown rice

Thoroughly blend mayonnaise and chutney. Combine with chicken, celery, onions, apple, grapes, pecans and rice. Serve chilled.

I usually use more chutney than it calls for. Everybody just loves this salad.

Sarah Jane Alston from The Junior League of Jackson's *Come On In* cookbook

DEVILED EGGS

hard boiled eggs

dill pickle relish

yellow mustard

mayonnaise

salt

pepper

Peel eggs, being careful not to tear them. Cut in half and put yolks in a mixing bowl. Mash yolks with fork. Add pickle relish, yellow mustard, salt and pepper, to taste. Add enough mayonnaise to hold the mixture together. Spoon or pipe this mixture into egg halves. Garnish with paprika, slice of green olive, sprig of dill or a small boiled shrimp.

An attractive alternative for this classic recipe is to cut the eggs in half across the short length rather than length-wise. Slice a tiny bit off the bottom of each half and they will stand up nicely on a platter. This is particularly helpful when you are serving a crowd.

Barefoot Contessa Ina Garten's method for boiling eggs is the best I have ever tried. She says to place your eggs in a saucepan and add enough cold water to cover. Bring the water to a boil and immediately turn off the heat. Let the eggs sit in the pan for 15 minutes. Remove eggs to a bowl and allow to rest for at least 2 minutes. When eggs are cool enough to handle, crack the eggs on each side and then roll them back and forth with your hand, breaking up the shell. Remove and discard the shell.

 Anne Robertson

EGG SALAD

6 free-range chicken eggs, hard boiled

1 Tablespoon fresh dill, finely chopped

1 Tablespoon fresh chives and/or green onions, finely chopped

mayonnaise, homemade or very good quality

salt

pepper

Peel six hard-boiled eggs; slice in half and place them face down on a platter. Gently mash with a fork into small pieces. You will know when they look right. Please do not put these eggs in a food processor. There is nothing worse than mushy egg salad.

Gently stir in dill, chives and/or green onions and a small amount mayonnaise—just enough to hold it all together. If I know all of the salad will be eaten in one meal, I use homemade mayonnaise. Add salt and pepper to taste. I like more pepper than salt.

Serve on buttered and toasted bread. Great with fresh tomatoes, too!

The beauty of this recipe is found in its fresh ingredients and simplicity. The quality and freshness of the eggs really, really matter. Eggs are, after all, the star of the show. If you can, go to the Farmers Market for free-range eggs. This color, flavor and texture cannot be found in the grocery store!

Phoebe Smith Porter

GRILLED STEAK SALAD

1½ pounds trimmed, boneless sirloin (1 inch thick) grilled (seasoned to your liking)

10 new potatoes, boiled and cooled, then halved

6 ounces haricots verts, blanched and cooled

1 red bell pepper, seeded and julienned

½ red onion, very thinly sliced

greens of your choice

DRESSING

1 large garlic clove

¼ teaspoon sugar

¼ teaspoon sea salt

2 teaspoons Dijon mustard

1½ Tablespoons minced fresh tarragon or ½ teaspoon dried

2 Tablespoons red wine vinegar

½ cup olive oil

Use blender or processor to mix the dressing. Thinly slice the sirloin. Line platter with greens. Toss potatoes, beans, pepper and onion with some of the dressing and arrange on top of greens. Fan sirloin atop veggies and drizzle remaining dressing on meat. Deviled eggs are a good accompaniment.

Julie Moore

CLASSIC SEAFOOD LOUIS

Crabmeat or boiled shrimp

Avocados

Bibb or other lettuce

Use any or all of the following:

Tomato wedges

Hard-boiled egg slices

Asparagus spears

Ripe olives

Place Bibb lettuce on individual salad plates; arrange crabmeat or shrimp and sliced avocados on the lettuce. Add one or more optional items to each plate. Pass Louis Dressing.

LOUIS DRESSING

1 cup mayonnaise

¼ cup chili sauce

¼ cup finely-chopped green pepper

2 Tablespoons thinly-sliced green onion with tops

1 teaspoon lemon juice

¼ teaspoon cayenne pepper

¼ cup whipping cream, whipped

Season to taste and mix together all ingredients except the whipped cream and chill thoroughly. When ready to serve, gently fold the whipped cream into the mix.

JoAnne Prichard Morris

CRAB SALAD *with* ASPARAGUS, AVOCADO AND LIME

1 pound asparagus, tough bottoms snapped off

1 pound fresh cooked crabmeat, picked for shell fragments

2 heads Bibb lettuce (about ½ pound)

2 ripe avocados, halved, pitted and peeled

1 ruby red grapefruit, peeled and cut into segments

LIME VINAIGRETTE

3 Tablespoons fresh lime juice

4 ½ teaspoons rice wine vinegar

2 teaspoons grated lime zest

salt and freshly-ground pepper

1½ teaspoons honey

3 Tablespoons olive oil

3 Tablespoons peanut oil

1½ teaspoons fresh ginger

Whisk together the lime juice, vinegar, lime zest, ginger and honey in a small bowl. Whisk in the oils. Season to taste with salt and pepper. Set aside.

Bring pot of water to boil and cook asparagus until just tender, about 5 minutes, then plunge into a bowl of ice water. When asparagus is cold, drain and toss with 3 tablespoons of the vinaigrette. Set aside.

Toss the crabmeat with 3 tablespoons of the vinaigrette and set aside. In a large bowl, toss the Bibb lettuce leaves with 3 tablespoons of the vinaigrette.

Divide the dressed Bibb lettuce leaves among four large chilled plates. Place an avocado half on top of the lettuce on each plate and drizzle with a little vinaigrette. Arrange a bundle of dressed asparagus next to each avocado half. Divide the dressed crabmeat among the plates, draping it over the avocado and the asparagus. Garnish with the grapefruit segments and serve.

This is an incredibly delicious salad. It's easier than it looks and makes a perfect summer dinner on Thursday nights when Mr. Dugan's truck is spotted.

Anne Robertson from her family cookbook *First You Need a Big Pot,* via Tom Douglas' *Seattle's Kitchen*

FRIED GREEN TOMATO AND GRILLED SHRIMP *with* BLACK-EYED PEA AND CORN SALSA

Serves 3-4

salad greens of your choice

3-4 slices green tomatoes, ½ inch thick

1 cup all-purpose flour

1 teaspoon salt

½ teaspoon pepper

1 large egg

½ cup buttermilk

2 cups panko bread crumbs

½ pound 31-40 count shrimp

Cajun seasoning, to taste

½ cup black-eyed peas

1 ear corn

2 Tablespoons red onion, finely diced

1 small Kirby cucumber, finely diced

1 jalapeno, finely diced

2 Tablespoons chopped cilantro

1 lime, juiced

1 Tablespoon extra virgin olive oil

2-3 strips bacon, cooked to desired crispness

½ cup feta cheese

AVOCADO GREEN GODDESS DRESSING

1 avocado, peeled, pit removed, and chopped

½ cup plain yogurt

½ cup sour cream

2 Tablespoons fresh parsley, chopped

2 Tablespoons fresh cilantro, chopped

2 Tablespoons scallions, green parts only, chopped

1 Tablespoon fresh tarragon, chopped

1 lemon, juiced

salt and pepper

Combine all Ingredients for dressing in a food processor or blender and pulse until combined and smooth.

Dredge green tomato slices in flour, salt, and pepper. Dip into buttermilk. Dredge in bread crumbs. Set aside.

Season shrimp with Cajun seasoning and grill in grill pan or cast iron skillet. Set aside.

Combine black-eyed peas, corn, red onion, cucumber, jalapeno, lime juice and olive oil in a separate bowl, and season to taste with salt and pepper. Fry green tomato slices in a deep fat fryer or skillet with ½ inch of peanut oil until golden brown. Set aside on paper towels to drain, and season with salt and pepper.

Serve tomato slices over salad greens, layered with black-eyed pea and corn salsa, shrimp, drizzled with dressing and topped with crumbled bacon and feta cheese.

Serenity Luckett from Nate Ballard,
a local Belhaven chef and great friend

COUNTY DOWN CURRIED SHRIMP SALAD

Serves 2-4

8 ounces frozen shrimp

2 teaspoons tomato paste

1-2 teaspoons lemon juice

1 teaspoon curry powder

4 heaping teaspoons mayonnaise

1 cup cooked rice

Hard-boiled egg

Cucumber, sliced

Tomato, sliced

Thoroughly defrost shrimp, or use fresh shrimp. Cook shrimp. Drain well. Mix tomato paste, lemon juice and curry powder into the mayonnaise. Fold in rice and shrimp. Divide and serve on large lettuce leaves. Garnish with sliced hard-boiled egg, cucumber and tomato.

Lynda Wright

LIME SHRIMP

Serves 4-6

1 pound large shrimp

Crab boil

5 fresh limes

1 teaspoon sea salt

3 envelopes Sweet'N Low or other sugar substitute

⅓ cup mayonnaise

1 cup sour cream

Cook shrimp using the juice and body of 1 lime in the crab boil water. Zest the other 4 limes into bowl and then squeeze juice from them. Add 2 envelopes of sugar substitute and dissolve in lime juice. Save the other envelope in case final dressing is too tart. The tartness of dressing will vary according to strength of limes and how much zest is used, and your own personal taste.

Stir in salt, mayonnaise and sour cream. Add cooked shrimp and chill for a minimum of 4 hours. Best made day before. Can be served over salad greens or used as an hors d' oeuvre.

Buddie Barksdale
via my sister, Melanie Williams

VIRGIE'S TUNA SALAD

Two small cans of albacore tuna—I prefer tuna packed in olive oil for its rich flavor

¼ cup red onion, finely chopped

1 clove of garlic, finely minced

½ of a small green or red bell pepper, finely chopped (whichever you have on hand)

1 small rib of celery, thinly sliced

4 Tablespoons coarsely chopped Italian olive salad (such as Boscoli or Central Grocery)

1 Tablespoon (or more) coarsely chopped capers

2 Tablespoons freshly-squeezed lemon juice

pinch of red pepper

pinch of sea salt

fresh-ground black pepper

¼ cup chopped fresh parsley

Drain the tuna well and place in a glass mixing bowl. Mix in remaining ingredients, except parsley, and place in the fridge for at least two hours to allow flavors to blend. If the salad becomes too dry, add a little olive oil and/or lemon juice just before serving, along with the fresh parsley.

This tuna salad is wonderful served as a sandwich on toasted bread or on a bed of lettuce. Tomatoes are a lovely accompaniment. I don't really have a recipe so the portions are more art than science. I first had something like this in Italy in 1987.

Virgie Lindsay

KAKOW'S CURRIED TUNA SALAD

1 can tuna

sesame seeds

¼-½ cup diced celery

¼ small onion, finely chopped

½ bell pepper, diced

1 teaspoon curry powder

1 teaspoon soy sauce

garlic salt, to taste

mayonnaise, just enough to hold the salad together.

Combine tuna, vegetables and sesame seeds. Mix mayonnaise with curry powder, soy sauce and garlic salt and stir into tuna mixture.

Anne Robertson

SEARED TUNA SALAD

Serves 2-3

½ head Chinese cabbage (Napa or Savoy), chopped

1 bunch watercress (ok to leave out)

¼ cup chopped fresh cilantro

1 English cucumber, sliced

2 green onions, sliced on the diagonal

2 radishes, sliced

1 carrot thinly sliced

¼ cup slivered almonds, toasted

½ can mandarin orange segments, drained

Ahi Tuna, seared (*see recipe below*)

GINGER VINAIGRETTE

3 Tablespoons low sodium soy sauce

Juice of 1 lime

2 teaspoons rice wine vinegar

2 teaspoons freshly-grated ginger

4 teaspoons Chinese mustard

1 Tablespoon honey

Freshly ground black pepper to taste

⅓ cup canola oil

1 Tablespoon sesame oil (less if using toasted sesame oil)

Mix first 7 dressing ingredients in small bowl, then drizzle in oils while whisking constantly. Set aside

Combine veggies, toss with some dressing. Divide onto 2-3 plates, place oranges and sprinkle almonds on top.

AHI TUNA

2 ahi tuna steaks, thawed but cold (frozen individually packaged from seafood department at McDade's work fine)

sesame oil

sea salt, ground white pepper

½ cup sesame seeds (less expensive if bought in Asian section of grocery if they have it)

1 Tablespoon canola oil

Rub both sides of tuna with salt, pepper and sesame oil. Press both sides into sesame seeds on a plate, sear in a cast iron skillet at high heat, 2-3 minutes on each side. You want it to be pink in the center. Slice and place atop the salad.

Beverly Fulcher

WHITE BEAN AND TUNA SALAD

1 can cannellini beans, drained and rinsed

4 Tablespoons extra virgin olive oil, divided

1 clove garlic, smashed with the flat of a knife

1 teaspoon chopped fresh rosemary

red chili flakes

1 can tuna packed in olive oil

6 ounces (half of one 12-ounce jar) pickled, crispy
carrots such as Tillen Farms brand, drained
and diced (can substitute 6 ounces peppadew
peppers)

1 Tablespoon capers, drained

4 cups baby arugula

juice of one lemon or to taste

salt and pepper to taste

Heat 2 tablespoons olive oil in a saucepan large
enough to hold the beans. Add the garlic, rosemary
and chile flakes and sauté gently (do not let garlic
brown) until the garlic and rosemary are very aro-
matic. Add the beans and stir gently, taking care not
to break up beans, until beans are warm.

   Remove from heat and turn into a salad bowl.
Add tuna, capers and carrots and stir gently to combine. Taste and add remaining olive oil, lemon juice
and salt and pepper to taste. Serve over arugula.

Margaret Cupples

Potatoes, Rice & Beans

MAZALEE'S POTATO SALAD

5 pounds russet potatoes

3 hard-boiled eggs, divided

salt and pepper

1 bunch green onions, finely chopped

½ bunch fresh parsley, finely chopped

1 cup diced celery

Boil potatoes, peel, and cut in ½-inch dice. Boil eggs, chop whites, and add to potatoes. Mash yolks with fork and reserve for dressing. Add chopped parsley, celery and green onion.

Salt the potato mixture heavily. It is almost impossible to add too much salt, but you need to taste it to be the judge. Season with ground black pepper to taste.

1 cup Hellman's mayonnaise

¼ cup yellow mustard

3 Tablespoons cider vinegar

mashed egg yolks

Mix dressing, fold into the potatoes, and taste. Correct seasoning. The potato salad isn't dry, or wet; if anything, it is firm. If too firm, make additional dressing with mayonnaise, mustard and vinegar.

My husband, Overton, grew up in Baton Rouge with his father's sister's family, which included Mazalee Burns, a pan-generational figure who provided love and guidance to the chillun' and delicious southern cooking for the family. Maz didn't measure, but this is the way she made her potato salad.

Marilyn Moore

HAM AND CHEESE POTATO SALAD *with* TANGY SHALLOT DRESSING

2 pounds small new potatoes, scrubbed

3 cups cubed cooked ham

2 cups coarsely shredded Swiss cheese

½ cup sun-dried tomatoes packed in oil, drained and cut into small strips

½ cup thinly-sliced green onions

3 Tablespoons chopped fresh parsley

1 Tablespoon chopped fresh dill

1 small head romaine lettuce, washed and dried

Extra sprigs of parsley for garnish

TANGY SHALLOT DRESSING

2 shallots, peeled and minced

½ cup dry white wine

¼ cup white wine (or cider) vinegar

1 cup mayonnaise

¼ cup chopped fresh parsley

3 Tablespoons chopped fresh tarragon

¼ cup chopped fresh dill

generous dash Tabasco

1 teaspoon Dijon mustard

Put the minced shallots for the dressing in a small non-reactive pan. Add the wine and vinegar and cook over high until the mixture is reduced to ¼ cup. Cool. Stir the shallot mixture into the mayonnaise along with the herbs, Tabasco and mustard. Chill until ready to serve.

Slice the potatoes about ¼-inch thick, leaving peel on. Place in a vegetable steamer and steam for 7 to 8 minutes or until fork tender. Remove to side dish and toss with ½ cup Tangy Shallot Dressing and allow to sit 30 minutes.

In a large bowl, gently toss together the potatoes, ham, cheese, tomatoes, onions, parsley and dill. Add remaining dressing and toss.

To serve, coarsely shred the romaine onto plates and spoon the ham salad over the top. Garnish with parsley. Serve at room temperature or chilled.

Betty Hise via friend Marilyn Harris, long-time Cincinnati radio food show host and a Mississippi native

CATHERINE SULLIVAN'S POTATO SALAD

new or red potatoes

olive oil

garlic, minced

mint, chopped

freshly-ground black pepper to taste

salt to taste

Preheat oven to 425°.

Quarter potatoes—use small tender ones. Place potatoes in shallow tray and sprinkle very lightly with olive oil. (Don't drench.) Roast in a shallow tray for about 1 hour, till tender (but not desiccated!) Toss by hand in a big bowl with lots of minced fresh garlic, chopped mint and good olive oil. Sprinkle with freshly-ground pepper and a small amount salt. Serve hot, cold or room temperature.

Great for a big crowd.

👑 Ginnie Munford via Catherine Sullivan

AMERICAN CAFÉ POTATO SALAD

Serves 6—8

2¼ pounds red wax potatoes

4 ounces white wine

1½ Tablespoons wine vinegar

1 Tablespoon, plus 1 teaspoon Dijon mustard

dash of salt and pepper

1½ teaspoons thyme

3 Tablespoons dill

3 Tablespoons parsley

¼ pound red onion, diced

8 ounces olive oil

Place potatoes in pot. Cover with cold water to which 1 Tablespoon salt has been added. Bring to boil and simmer 12 -16 minutes or until tender. Drain in colander and set aside.

In a mixing bowl, place all the remaining ingredients except the olive oil and onions. Whisk together about 30 seconds. While still whisking, slowly pour in the olive oil until it is incorporated. When the potatoes are just cool enough to handle, cut them into bite-sized pieces and drop them in the sauce. Add onions. Serve warm or refrigerate.

👑 Rebecca Wiggs

NEW POTATO SALAD

1½ pounds new potatoes, boiled just till done, don't overcook

DRESSING
½ cup olive oil

½ cup dry vermouth

1 Tablespoon minced shallots

¼ cup minced mint

1 clove garlic, minced

1 teaspoon salt

½ teaspoon pepper

Mix dressing ingredients. Pour over potatoes, toss and refrigerate.

 Julie Moore

SWEET POTATO SALAD

4 large sweet potatoes

1 Tablespoon Dijon mustard

¼ cup cider vinegar

¼ cup honey

⅓ cup dried currants

⅓ cup cooking oil

⅔ cup red onions, diced

½ cup dried cranberries

⅔ cup pecans, chopped

Scrub, boil, peel and dice the sweet potatoes. Mix remaining ingredients, except pecans, for the dressing. Season to taste and toss dressing with potatoes. Refrigerate. Garnish with the chopped pecans.

Claire Barksdale

PINEAPPLE-SWEET POTATO SALAD

Serves 8

4 small sweet potatoes

¼ cup mayonnaise

1 Tablespoon mustard

4 celery stalks, sliced ¼-inch thick

1 small red bell pepper, cut into ¼-inch dice

1 cup diced fresh pineapple

2 scallions, finely chopped

salt and pepper

½ cup coarsely chopped toasted pecans

chopped fresh chives

Preheat oven to 400°. Wrap each sweet potato in foil and bake for 1 hour. Unwrap; let cool. Peel, cut into ¾-inch chunks.

In a large bowl, mix mayonnaise and mustard. Add sweet potatoes, celery, bell pepper, pineapple, and scallions; toss gently. Season to taste with salt and pepper. Cover and refrigerate about 1 hour.

Fold in pecans and sprinkle with chives.

Betty Hise

APRICOT BULGHUR PILAF

2 Tablespoons olive oil

1½ cups chopped onions

1½ cups bulghur

2¼ cups boiling water

½ cup chopped dried apricots

1½ Tablespoons minced fresh spearmint leaves
(2 tsp. dried)

2 Tablespoons chopped fresh dill (1½ tsp. dried)

½ cup chopped fresh parsley

juice of 1 lemon

salt and ground black pepper to taste

1 tomato, cut into wedges

lemon wedges

½ cup grated feta cheese (optional, but you may want to use less salt if you do use the feta)

Heat the oil in a saucepan and sauté the onions for 3 minutes. Stir in the bulghur and sauté for 2 more minutes. Add the boiling water, cover and bring back to a boil. Reduce heat and gently simmer 10 minutes.

Add the apricots without stirring them in, cover and cook for another 5 to 10 minutes, until the water is absorbed and the bulghur is fluffy. Stir in the mint, dill, parsley and lemon juice. Add salt and pepper to taste.

Serve garnished with wedges of fresh tomato and lemon, and top with grated feta if you like.

Carol Taff, reprinted with permission of the author from *Moosewood Restaurant Cooks at Home*, Copyright © 1994 Moosewood, Inc., Simon & Schuster Publishers, New York, New York.

ARTICHOKE-RICE SALAD

Serves 6-8

- 1 package chicken-flavored Rice-a-Roni
- 4 green onions, chopped or sliced thin
- ½ bell pepper, chopped
- 12 stuffed olives, sliced
- 2 (6-ounce) jars artichoke hearts
- ½ teaspoon curry powder
- ⅓ cup mayonnaise

Cook Rice-a-Roni as directed on package, omitting butter. Cool in large bowl. Add green onions, pepper and olives. Drain artichokes and cut into quarters. Reserve the liquid and combine with curry powder and mayonnaise. Add artichokes to rice and mix well. Add dressing (may not need all of it) and mix. Chill.

The recipe says to chill for 24 hours, but that really isn't necessary. It does get better as the flavors blend, however, and can obviously be made ahead of time if planning a gathering. Also easy to double.

Walterine Odom

CHARLOTTE CAPERS' RICE SALAD

- 2 cups raw rice, cooked in chicken broth
- 2 (6.5- to 7-ounce) jars marinated artichoke hearts chopped (reserve liquid)
- 2 green onions, chopped
- 1 bell pepper, chopped
- ⅓ cup Hellman's mayo
- ¼ teaspoon curry powder
- 12 stuffed, sliced olives, optional

Blend mayonnaise, curry and marinade from artichokes. Put all together. Add olives, if you wish.

You don't want the rice to be mushy, so I use Uncle Ben's or Basmati rice and cut the cooking liquid by about ¼.

Betty Allin via Charlotte Capers

WILD RICE SALAD RING

1½ cups wild rice

1½ cups long grain rice, washed

1 Tablespoon salt

2 Tablespoons butter

1 cup diced green pepper

1 cup diced celery

½ cup finely chopped scallions

½ cup finely chopped parsley

In a large saucepan, bring 6 quarts water and salt to boil. Sprinkle in wild rice and boil it over moderately high heat for 7 minutes. Sprinkle long grain rice into the wild rice and cook it for 18 minutes. Drain rice. Add butter and stir the rice until the grains are coated.

Set colander of rice over a pan of boiling water, cover with a cloth and steam the rice over medium high heat for 15 or twenty minutes, or until it is dry. Turn the rice out into a large bowl, fluff it with a long-tined fork, and let it stand for 20 minutes.

Add to the rice: about 1 cup French Dressing, green peppers, celery, scallions and parsley. Toss the mixture and season with salt and freshly-ground pepper. Pack the rice into a 6-cup mold, lightly oiled.

Just before serving, unmold the rice onto a round platter and garnish with rings of green peppers. Serve at room temperature.

FRENCH DRESSING

¼ cup white wine vinegar

1 teaspoon dry Dijon-style mustard

½ teaspoon salt

¼ teaspoon freshly-ground black pepper

2 Tablespoons shallot, chopped very fine

¾ cup olive oil

In a bowl whisk together the vinegar, salt, shallot, mustard and pepper. Add oil in steady stream, whisking until emulsified. Makes 1 cup dressing.

Good with boiled shrimp, which you can serve in the center of the ring. Pass extra French Dressing.

JoAnne Prichard Morris

JAMAICAN RICE SALAD

1½ cups Basmati rice, uncooked

2 celery stalks, finely chopped

1 red bell pepper, finely chopped

3 or 4 green onions, finely chopped

½ cup Roses lime juice

1 ⅓ Tablespoons Indian curry powder

2 Tablespoons white wine vinegar

1 teaspoon salt

½ teaspoon cayenne pepper

½ cup extra virgin olive oil

½ cup whole cashews

romaine lettuce

Cook rice and set aside in colander to drain. Toss cooled rice with everything, except cashews, in large bowl. Set aside in refrigerator for an hour or two or overnight.

Serve in a large bowl over bed of romaine lettuce with cashews on top.

Kathy Lyell

WINNING RICE SALAD

3 cups cooked rice (leftovers are perfect)

2 Tablespoons chopped scallions

2 Tablespoons chopped parsley

1 green onion, chopped

½ cucumber, seeded and chopped (peeled or unpeeled)

4-5 radishes, sliced

dash or 2 of Tabasco, optional

DRESSING
½ cup olive oil

¼ cup white vinegar

1 clove garlic, crushed

1 Tablespoon Dijon mustard

salt and pepper, to taste

Whisk dressing ingredients together. Remove garlic.

Mix rice and other salad ingredients, except Tabasco, in a large bowl. Pour in ½ cup of dressing and mix well. Add Tabasco, if using, and more dressing if needed. Chill 1 hour before serving.

 Rebecca Wiggs

MAMA'S HOPPIN' JOHN SALAD

Serves 8

- ½ cup uncooked long-grain rice
- 2 cups fresh or frozen black-eyed peas
- 2 teaspoons salt, divided
- ¼ cup fresh lemon juice
- 2 Tablespoons olive oil
- 1 jalapeno pepper, seeded and minced
- 1 garlic clove, pressed
- ¼ teaspoon pepper
- ½ cup chopped celery
- ½ cup loosely-packed fresh parsley leaves, chopped
- ¼ cup loosely-packed fresh mint leaves, chopped

Prepare rice according to package directions. Cook peas with 1 teaspoon salt in water to cover in large saucepan over medium-high heat stirring often, 30 minutes or until tender, drain.

Whisk together lemon juice, next 4 ingredients, and remaining 1 teaspoon of salt in a large bowl. Stir in peas, rice, celery, parsley and mint until blended. Cover and chill at least 2 hours. Season with salt to taste.

This and the Marinated Corn Bean Salad are my favorite salad recipes from my mama's kitchen. She has had them for over 40 years and can't remember the source! Perfect for the Summer!

Rachel Misener from her mother, Sharon Busler

LOUISA'S HOPPIN' JOHN SALAD

- 2 cups dried black-eyed peas (cook, drain, and rinse) or four 15-ounce cans (drain and rinse)
- 1 cup cooked rice
- 1 red bell pepper, diced
- 1 bunch scallions with green tops, chopped
- 10 ounces diced ham (optional)
- mint, chopped (optional)

DRESSING

- ½ cup rice wine vinegar
- 1 cup extra virgin olive oil
- 2 Tablespoons chipotle pepper puree
- ½ cup molasses
- salt and pepper

Whisk vinegar, oil, pepper and molasses for dressing and set aside. Combine peas, rice, ham, scallions, red pepper and toss with dressing, adding mint, if desired.

Louisa Dixon

GRILLED CORN AND BUTTER BEAN SALAD

1 (16-ounce) package frozen butter beans; fresh may be used

4 ears fresh corn, husk removed

1 large red onion, cut into thick slices

1 large red bell pepper, cut into thick rings

¾ cup mayonnaise

3 Tablespoons chopped fresh basil

1 clove garlic, pressed

1 teaspoon salt

1 teaspoon Worcestershire sauce

½ teaspoon freshly-ground black pepper

1 cup grape tomatoes, cut in half

Cook butter beans according to the package directions; drain and cool completely.

Meanwhile, preheat grill to 350-400° heat (medium-high). Grill corn, covered with grill lid, 15 minutes or until done, turning every 4 to 5 minutes. Some kernels will begin to char and pop. At the same time, grill onion and bell pepper, 5 minutes on each side or until tender.

Cool all vegetables completely. Cut kernels from cobs. Chop onion and bell pepper into ½ inch pieces.

Stir together mayonnaise and next 5 ingredients. Stir in tomatoes, corn kernels, onion and pepper pieces. Add salt to taste.

My family has loved this recipe. It really captures the taste of summer in Mississippi.

Beth Graham

BUTTER BEAN SALAD

2 packages frozen baby limas.

½-¾ cup toasted almond slices

½ cup olive oil

¼ cup balsamic vinegar

½ cup crumbled feta cheese

1 bunch green onions, chopped

2 cloves garlic, pressed

4 ounce can ripe olive slices, drained

1 Tablespoon fresh cilantro, chopped

½ green bell pepper, chopped

½ red bell pepper, chopped

½ cup mayonnaise

salt and pepper to taste

Cook and drain lima beans.

Combine remaining ingredients and toss beans with the dressing.

This is very good warm, just made. Very good chilled, too!

Mary Nichols

LIMA BEAN HUMMUS

Makes 4 cups

2 (10-ounce) packages frozen baby limas

1 large onion, chopped

5 garlic cloves, smashed

1 teaspoon salt

¼ cup fresh cilantro, chopped

¼ cup chopped fresh flat-leaf parsley (I've used curly-leafed Italian parsley)

1 teaspoon ground cumin

¼ teaspoon cayenne, or to taste

3 Tablespoons fresh lemon juice, or more to taste

5 Tablespoons extra virgin olive oil

2 Tablespoons fresh dill, chopped

2 Tablespoons fresh mint, chopped

freshly-ground black pepper

Combine beans, onion, garlic, salt with water to cover in a 3-quart saucepan and simmer, covered, until beans are tender, about 8 minutes. Stir in cilantro and parsley, then remove from heat and let stand, uncovered, for 5 minutes. Drain.

Transfer bean mixture to a food processor; add cumin, cayenne, lemon juice, dill, mint, 4 tablespoons (¼ cup) of the oil, and puree until smooth. Transfer to a bowl and cool to room temperature, stirring occasionally.

Season dip with salt, pepper and lemon juice to taste. Mound in a serving bowl and drizzle with remaining 1 tablespoon oil.

Serve with pita toasts (made by brushing pita bread with olive oil and toasting in the oven), bagel chips, or wheat thins. Also, pita chips (like Stacey's brand) work well.

Von Jicka

SALADE ROUGE

Serves 5-6

- 1 pound can red kidney beans, drained
- 6 ounces cooked beets, peeled and cubed
- 6 ounces red cabbage, shredded
- 3 Tablespoons vegetable oil
- 1 Tablespoon tarragon vinegar
- 1 teaspoon ground cumin
- salt and freshly-ground black
- 1 small radicchio or other red leaf lettuce
- 1 small red onion, sliced

Combine the beans, beets and red cabbage in a bowl. Add the oil, vinegar, cumin, salt and pepper. Mix well.

Line a shallow glass bowl with the lettuce leaves. Pile the beans, beets and cabbage into the center. Top with red onion slices.

 Susan Johnson

CORN AND EDAMAME SUCCOTASH

- 1½ cups frozen or fresh shelled edamame
- 1 Tablespoon red bell pepper, chopped
- ¼ cup onion, chopped
- 2 cloves garlic, minced
- 2 cups fresh corn kernels
- 3 Tablespoons dry white wine or water
- 2 Tablespoons rice vinegar
- 3 Tablespoons fresh basil, chopped or 1 teaspoon dried basil
- ½ teaspoon salt, or to taste
- freshly-ground pepper, to taste

Cook edamame in a large saucepan of lightly salted water until tender, about 4 minutes or according to package directions. Drain well.

Heat oil in a large nonstick skillet over medium-high heat. Add bell pepper, onion and garlic; cook, stirring frequently, until vegetables start to soften, about 2 minutes. Stir in corn, wine (or water) and the edamame; cook stirring frequently, for 4 minutes. Remove from the heat. Stir in vinegar, parsley, basil, salt and pepper. Serve Immediately.

Nancy Lawrence

EDAMAME SALAD

Serves 8

  2 bags frozen shelled edamame

  1 can sweet corn

  2 cans black beans

  4 tomatoes

  1 bunch flat-leaf parsley

  salt and pepper

Thaw edamame. Rinse and drain black beans and sweet corn. Finely chop tomatoes and parsley. In a bowl mix edamame, black beans, corn, tomatoes and parsley. Salt and pepper to taste.

Virginia Farr

MEXICAN CORN SALSA

  1 can white corn, drained and rinsed

  1 can black beans, drained and rinsed

  1 can Rotel tomatoes

  ½ minced jalapeno pepper

  ½ small onion, minced

  Juice of 1 lime

Mix together and chill. Serve with tortilla Scoops.

Margaret Ann Forester

LIBBA'S BLACK BEAN SALAD

2 (15-ounce) cans yellow corn, drained

2 (15-ounce) cans black beans, drained and rinsed

1 cup celery, finely chopped

1 red bell pepper, finely chopped

1 small red onion, finely chopped

1 bunch of cilantro, finely chopped

DRESSING

½ cup vegetable oil

3 Tablespoons Dijon mustard

¼ cup fresh lime juice

2 Tablespoons brown sugar

Stir together corn, black beans, celery, red pepper, onion and cilantro. Mix dressing well, then add to above mixture. Best chilled for at least 2 hours. Add salt to taste.

Libba Wilkes

MOTHER'S BLACK BEAN SALAD

1 (15-ounce) can black beans, rinsed and drained

1 cup seeded, chopped tomato

½ cup green pepper, chopped

½ cup purple onion, chopped

¼ cup fresh cilantro, finely chopped

1 can shoe peg corn, drained

1 jalapeno pepper, finely chopped

DRESSING

1 Tablespoon corn oil

juice of large lime

¼ teaspoon salt

½ teaspoon cumin

Mix all dressing ingredients. Blend dressing into salad/salsa and serve either on chopped lettuce or with tortilla chips.

This makes my mouth water just thinking about it.

Donna Barksdale

ITALIAN WHITE BEAN SALAD

Serves 4

1 (15.5 ounce) can cannellini beans, drained and rinsed

½ cup diced red onion (about ½ medium onion)

1 medium red or yellow bell pepper, seeded and diced

1 ripe red tomato, seeded and diced

1 large orange, peeled, membranes removed, seeded and diced

¼ cup fresh flat-leaf parsley, chopped

1 Tablespoon fresh chives, thinly-sliced

1 teaspoon fresh rosemary, finely minced

½ teaspoon kosher salt, or to taste

¼ teaspoon freshly-ground black pepper, or to taste

DRESSING

2 Tablespoons balsamic vinegar

2 to 3 cloves garlic, minced

⅛ teaspoon granulated sugar, or to taste

¼ cup extra virgin olive oil

salt and freshly-ground black pepper, to taste

Whisk together the vinegar, garlic and sugar in a small mixing bowl; slowly drizzle in the oil, whisking constantly and vigorously to emulsify. Taste and adjust the seasoning as necessary with salt, pepper and sugar; set aside until needed.

Combine the beans, onion, bell pepper, tomato, orange, parsley, chives and rosemary in a medium mixing bowl. Add the dressing and toss to coat. Season to taste with salt and pepper.

Make at least one hour (and up to 12 hours) before serving to allow the flavors to meld. Serve lightly chilled or at room temperature to accompany grilled seafood, chicken or pork.

Very tasty—great with tuna!

Kathy Woodliff via the Viking Cooking School

SPICY MIXED BEAN SALAD

Serves 8-10

- 1 pound can each of black beans, pinto beans, and red kidney beans
- 2 cups celery, chopped
- 1 large sweet salad onion (Vidalia or Red Spanish)
- 12 cherry tomatoes
- 1 large cucumber
- 1 or 2 medium to large fresh jalapeno peppers, to taste
- ¼ cup fresh cilantro, chopped
- ½ cup extra virgin olive oil

DRESSING
- 1 large clove garlic
- ½ teaspoon chili powder
- ½ teaspoon salt
- 1 teaspoon sugar, to taste
- generous dash Tabasco sauce
- ¼ cup red wine or cider vinegar

Finely mince the garlic and whisk into the olive oil along with the chili powder, salt, sugar and Tabasco. Whisk in the vinegar until well blended.

Place beans in colander, rinse and drain thoroughly. Move to a large bowl and gently toss in the celery.

Chop the onion and halve the cherry tomatoes. Peel, cut in half lengthwise, and seed the cucumber. Cut into thin slices. Seed and finely chop the jalapeno peppers. Toss onion, tomatoes, cucumber, jalapenos and cilantro into bean mixture.

Pour dressing over bean mixture and gently toss.

Betty Hise via friend Marilyn Harris, long-time Cincinnati radio food show host and a Mississippi native.

Greens & Vegetables

continued...

LOUIS PAPPAS' FAMOUS GREEK SALAD *with* GRANDMA DOT'S ANCHOVY DRESSING AND ANNIE LAURIE'S POTATO SALAD

1 large head of lettuce

3 cups of potato salad (special recipe below)

2 tomatoes cut into 6 wedges (more if you like)

1 cucumber, peeled and cut lengthwise into 8 fingers (use more cucumber if you like)

1 avocado, peeled and cut into wedges

4 portions of feta

1 green bell pepper cut into 8 rings

4 slices of canned or pickled beets (although I don't believe I've ever used those on this salad)

handful of shrimp or more

handful of anchovy fillets or less

12 black olive or more

4 whole green onions

Line a large round platter with lettuce leaves. Place 3 cups of potato salad in the center of the platter. Cover potato salad with remaining shredded lettuce. Place tomato wedges around outer edge of salad with a few on top. Place cucumbers between the tomatoes, making a solid base for the salad. Place the avocado slices around the outside of the salad. Arrange the slices of feta on top of the salad, as well as the green pepper, beets, shrimp, anchovy, olives and green onion. Cover salad with Dot Palmer's Salad Dressing—tastiest dressing ever!

ANNIE LAURIES POTATO SALAD

2 pounds of Idaho potatoes

1 large sweet onion, finely chopped

3 Tablespoons of red wine vinegar

2 teaspoons salt

1 cup mayonnaise

Boil and chop potatoes; pour vinegar over potatoes while still hot and let the potatoes soak up the vinegar, then mix in the rest of the ingredients.

DOT PALMER'S ANCHOVY DRESSING

6 tablespoons of olive oil

3 tablespoons of red wine vinegar

1 teaspoon of mustard

1 teaspoon of garlic or one clove

1 teaspoon of anchovy paste

salt and pepper

Mix and refrigerate.

This is gonna take a minute, but it's worth it! Enjoy!

Kelley Williams

JICAMA-ROMAINE SALAD

1 large head romaine lettuce

½ cup pecan halves or large pieces

2 medium jicama, julienned (approximately 1 cup)

3 oranges, peeled and sections removed

12 chives, snipped

TEQUILA-ORANGE VINAIGRETTE

¼ cup orange juice, freshly-squeezed

2 Tablespoons tequila

1 Tablespoon fruit-flavored or white wine vinegar

½ shallot

½ cup vegetable oil

¼ cup olive oil

salt

white pepper

Wash and dry lettuce. Tear leaves into bite-size pieces. Toast nuts on baking sheet for 10 to 12 minutes in 350° oven. Stir once or twice while toasting. Set aside. Peel and julienne jicama.

Place the orange juice, tequila, vinegar and shallot in a blender and blend or process at high speed. Slowly add the oils while still blending. Season with the salt and pepper.

Lightly toss the romaine and pecans. Arrange on a salad plate, distributing orange sections equally. Toss the jicama with some of the dressing and mound in the middle of each plate. Ladle the rest of the dressing onto each plate and sprinkle with chives.

Jicama, a root vegetable with a sweet, nutty flavor, is often referred to as a "Mexican potato," and is similar in texture to a water chestnut. This presentation is beautiful. However, this salad is every bit as tasty if all ingredients are tossed with dressing and served at once.

Nancy Lawrence

CRUNCHY ROMAINE TOSS

Serves 10-12

- 1 cup walnuts, chopped
- 1 package ramen noodles, uncooked, broken up (discard flavor packet)
- 4 Tablespoons unsalted butter
- 1 bunch broccoli, coarsely chopped
- 1 head romaine lettuce, washed, broken into pieces
- 1 cup Sweet and Sour Dressing

SWEET AND SOUR DRESSING

- 1 cup vegetable oil
- 1 cup sugar, or to taste
- ½ cup wine vinegar
- 3 teaspoons soy sauce
- Salt and pepper

Brown walnuts and noodles in butter; cool on paper towels. Combine noodles and walnuts with broccoli, romaine, and onions. Blend dressing ingredients, pour over salad and toss to coat well.

Variation: Steam broccoli in microwave 3-4 minutes before adding to salad. An "over-the-counter" dressing substitute is Brianna's Raspberry Vinaigrette.

Ellen Elise Treadway from The Junior League of Jackson's *Come On In* cookbook

SPINACH APRICOT SALAD

- 3 bags baby spinach
- ½ red onion, thinly sliced
- ½ cup dried apricots, chopped
- 1 cup feta cheese, crumbled
- 1 ripe avocado, chopped
- 2 (11-ounce) cans mandarin oranges, drained well on paper towels (squeeze lightly)

DRESSING

- ½ cup olive oil
- ½ cup canola oil
- ¼ cup white wine vinegar
- ¼ cup orange juice
- ¼ cup apricot jam
- 1 teaspoon salt
- 1½ teaspoon coriander
- ¼ teaspoon black pepper
- 2 Tablespoons chopped, dried apricots

Puree dressing ingredients in a blender. Mix salad ingredients. Toss together. (You may not need all of the dressing.)

Julie Moore

SALADE PARMESAN

Serves 8-10

- 5 Tablespoons Parmesan cheese, freshly-grated and divided
- ¼ cup olive or salad oil
- 2 Tablespoons fresh lemon juice
- 1 teaspoon dry mustard
- ½ teaspoon cracked black pepper
- 2 cloves garlic, minced
- dash of salt
- 10-12 cups torn salad greens
- croutons, crumbled goat cheese, broken walnuts and/or balsamic vinegar (optional)

Make ahead of time by mixing the dressing (first 7 ingredients) in the bowl and letting the lettuce sit on top unmixed until serving time.

Just before serving, add optional ingredients, toss well, sprinkle with remaining Parmesan cheese.

Kathryn McCraney from *Heart and Soul*
by the Junior League of Memphis

TOASTED ALMOND SALAD

- 2 heads Romaine lettuce, torn
- 1 pint cherry tomatoes
- 2 packages slivered almonds, toasted
- 1 cup Swiss cheese, grated
- ½ cup Parmesan, grated
- 4-5 slices bacon, crumbled

Layer in a large bowl. Cover and refrigerate for 24 hours.

DRESSING

- 3 large cloves of garlic, mashed
- ½ cup oil
- 1 teaspoon salt
- 1 lemon, juice only

Mix all together and let stand covered at least 3 hours. Add dressing to salad and toss before serving.

Ellen Treadway

TOASTED SEED SALAD

Serves 8-10

1 head Boston lettuce, torn

½ head romaine lettuce, torn

½ head red leaf lettuce, torn

½ cup carrot, grated

2 Tablespoons sesame seeds, toasted*

2 Tablespoons pumpkin seeds, toasted*

2 Tablespoons sunflower seeds, toasted and shelled*

2 Tablespoons almonds, sliced or slivered and toasted *

1 ounce (¼ cup) Parmesan or Romano cheese, freshly-grated

1 Roma tomato, diced

1 avocado, pitted, peeled and diced

DRESSING

2 Tablespoons fresh lemon juice

Dash Tabasco Sauce

⅛ teaspoon dry mustard

¼ teaspoon salt

2-3 cloves garlic, minced

¼ cup vegetable oil

Combine lemon juice, Tabasco, dry mustard, salt and garlic in a small bowl. Whisk in oil. Cover and chill.

Toss all lettuce in a salad bowl. Sprinkle in carrots, seeds, almonds and Parmesan. Add tomatoes and avocado. Pour dressing over salad and toss to coat. Serve immediately.

*Toast seeds in ungreased skillet over medium-high heat, stirring 2-3 minutes until golden. Or spread in a pan and toast in oven at 350°. Watch closely as seeds can burn quickly. Toasting seeds intensifies their flavor.

Claire Barksdale

LAYERED SALAD

Serves 15-20

- ½ bowl lettuce (shredded like cabbage)
- ½ cup each celery, bell pepper, onion, chopped and mixed together
- 1 can LeSeur peas, drained
- 1 pint mayonnaise (can use less) sprinkled with 2 Tablespoons sugar
- 6 ounces cheddar cheese, grated
- ¼ cup Parmesan cheese, grated
- 8 strips bacon, fried and crumbled

Layer ingredients in order. Do not toss! Cover and refrigerate for at least 8 hours (overnight is best).

Chopped eggs can be added before serving, if desired. Lasts for days in refrigerator.

Chyrl Grubbs

KATHERINE'S MANDARIN ORANGE SALAD

Serves 8

- 4 heads Bibb lettuce, torn
- 1 bunch watercress
- 2 (11-ounce) cans mandarin oranges, drained
- ½ cup slivered almonds, toasted

DRESSING

- 1 teaspoon dry mustard
- 1 teaspoon salt
- pepper
- ½ teaspoon Worcestershire sauce
- ½ cup salad oil
- ¼ cup sugar
- ¼ cup tarragon vinegar
- 2 teaspoons parsley, minced
- 1 red onion, thinly sliced

Combine all dressing ingredients and refrigerate for at least two hours.

Shake dressing and pour over lettuce and watercress. Toss oranges and slivered almonds with greens. Serve Immediately.

Katherine Wells from *Jacksonville and Company*, by the Junior League of Jacksonville, Florida,

MEREDITH'S MANDARIN ORANGE SALAD

1 can mandarin oranges, drained

1 head romaine or red leaf lettuce

½ cup green onion, chopped

½ cup celery, chopped

3¾ ounces slivered almonds, candied

DRESSING

¼ cup red wine vinegar

1 Tablespoon sugar

½ cup salad oil

2-3 drops Tabasco sauce

Pinch of salt and pepper

Prepare lettuce, onions, celery and oranges. Mix dressing ingredients.

To candy almonds, place almonds in skillet, add 2 tablespoons sugar and stir over moderate heat until sugar melts and coats almonds.

Toss salad just before serving.

A nice touch is to buy a package of wontons. Before serving the salad, deep fry wontons (one for each serving), pressing the center of each with a spoon to form a "bowl". Fill each fried wonton with the salad.

Also, adding sliced strawberries to the salad is good.

Meredith May

SEVEN-LAYER SALAD

1 large head of lettuce, broken (5 cups)

1 cup celery, sliced

1 cup green peppers or radishes, sliced

1 10-ounce package frozen green peas

3 hard-boiled eggs, sliced

1½ cup mayonnaise, more or less

3 Tablespoons Parmesan cheese

½ pound bacon, crumbled

Cook green peas for 1 minute. In large glass bowl or casserole, layer ingredients in order. Cover and chill up to 24 hours. Do not toss.

Mary Zimmerman

SPINACH-APPLE SALAD *with* MAPLE-CIDER VINAIGRETTE

1 (10-ounce) package fresh spinach

1 Gala apple, sliced

1 small red onion, sliced

1 (4-ounce) pack of goat cheese, crumbled

SUGAR CURRIED PECANS

1 (6-ounce) pack of pecan halves

2 Tablespoons butter, melted

3 Tablespoons sugar

¼ teaspoon ground ginger

⅛ teaspoon curry

⅛ teaspoon salt

⅛ teaspoon ground red pepper

MAPLE-CIDER VINAIGRETTE

⅓ cup cider vinegar

2 Tablespoons maple syrup

1 Tablespoon Dijon mustard

¼ teaspoon salt

¼ teaspoon pepper

⅔ cup olive oil

Preheat oven to 350°. Toss pecans in butter. Stir sugar and spices in bowl. Add pecans, tossing to coat. Spread on foil-lined pan. Bake 10-13 minutes or until toasted. Cool for 20 minutes.

Whisk vinaigrette ingredients, adding olive oil last. Mix together spinach, apple, onion and cheese crumbles and toss with dressing and pecans.

Stacy Underwood

STRAWBERRY FIELDS

4 cups mixed field greens

1 cup strawberries, hulled and halved

1 medium jicama, peeled and julienned

¼ cup roasted pistachios, chopped

DRESSING

1 cup strawberries, hulled and halved

2 Tablespoons raspberry vinegar

2 Tablespoons brown sugar, firmly packed

¼ cup olive oil

½ teaspoon fresh lemon juice

coarse salt

freshly-ground pepper

Process dressing ingredients in a food processor or blender until smooth, adding salt and pepper to taste. Set aside.

Combine greens, strawberries and jicama in a salad bowl. Just before serving, toss with dressing and sprinkle with pistachios.

👑 Bettye Jolly

STRAWBERRY SPINACH SALAD

¼ cup canola oil

2 Tablespoons white balsamic vinegar

2 Tablespoons honey

¼ teaspoon paprika

½ cup red onion, thinly sliced

10 ounces fresh baby spinach

1 quart strawberries, cleaned, hulled and sliced

¼ cup almonds, blanched and slivered

In a medium bowl, whisk together the canola oil, white balsamic vinegar, honey and paprika. Cover and chill.

In a large bowl, combine the onions, spinach, strawberries and almonds. Pour dressing over salad, and toss.

Emmie King

SPINACH, PEAR AND FRISEE' SALAD *with* SMOKED BACON

Serves 6

½ pound bacon

12 cups loosely-packed spinach leaves

6 cups loosely-packed frisee (also called curly endive)

⅔ cup red onions, thinly sliced

3 pears, halved, cored and thinly sliced

6 small bunches grapes

¼ cup Curried Cashews

HONEY SESAME VINAIGRETTE

3 Tablespoons white wine vinegar

3 Tablespoons Dijon mustard

2 Tablespoons honey

kosher salt

freshly-ground pepper

1 teaspoon garlic, minced

3 Tablespoons sesame seeds, toasted

½ cup peanut oil

Whisk together the vinegar, mustard, honey, sesame seeds, garlic and salt and pepper to taste in bowl. Gradually whisk in the oil. Set aside.

Cook bacon until crisp, 8-10 minutes. Cut the slices into 1-inch pieces. Keep the bacon warm. In a large bowl, combine the spinach, frisee, red onions and sliced pears. Toss with enough vinaigrette to coat everything well.

Divide the salad among 6 plates. Garnish each salad with pieces of warm bacon and spiced cashews. Set a grape cluster on the side of each plate. The bacon can be cooked ahead, stored in the refrigerator, and reheated. The cashews can be cooked early in the day and stored at room temperature. The vinaigrette can be refrigerated, tightly covered, for several days.

CURRIED CASHEWS

¼ cup cashews

1 Tablespoon butter, melted

⅛ teaspoon cayenne or more

1 teaspoon curry powder

1 teaspoon brown sugar

½ teaspoon kosher salt

1 teaspoon rosemary, chopped

Toast the cashews until golden, 8-10 minutes in 400° oven. Meanwhile, combine the melted butter, rosemary, curry powder, brown sugar, salt and cayenne in a bowl. Add the toasted cashews while they are still hot and toss with a rubber spatula so they are thoroughly coated with the spices and butter.

Anne Robertson in her family cookbook *First You Need a Big Pot*, via Tom Douglas' *Seattle Kitchen*

THE THANKSGIVING SALAD

1 bunch spinach torn into small pieces

6 slices crispy bacon, crumbled

½ cup shredded Jarlsberg cheese

¼ cup chopped walnuts

DRESSING

½ cup sugar

½ cup white vinegar

2 Tablespoons salad oil

1 Tablespoon chopped green onion

1 Tablespoon parsley, snipped finely

1 teaspoon Worcestershire

1 teaspoon Dijon mustard

cracked pepper—I like more, others less

Place dressing ingredients in jar or salad cruet. Shake well and chill. Combine salad ingredients and toss with dressing.

Susan Garrard

SPINACH SALAD with POPPY SEED DRESSING

Serves 15-20

2 bunches spinach

½ head iceberg lettuce

1 cup dried cranberries

½ cup slivered almonds, toasted

2-3 Fuji or Gala apples, diced

⅔ cup Swiss cheese, cubed

½ to 1 pound bacon, cooked crisp, crumbled

¼-½ red onion, diced

POPPY SEED DRESSING

1 cup red wine vinegar with garlic

1 cup vegetable oil

1 cup sugar

2 Tablespoons poppy seeds

1 Tablespoon salt

Make dressing night before. This recipe is enough for two salads. To double, add more spinach, iceberg, almonds, cheese and onions.

I used one box of baby spinach from Sam's. Two boxes of baby spinach plus iceberg would serve many more.

Sara Margaret Johnson

SPINACH, LENTIL AND ROASTED SWEET POTATO SALAD
with POMEGRANATE VINAIGRETTE

Serves 4

1 medium sweet potato, peeled and diced into
¼-inch pieces

1 Tablespoon extra virgin olive oil

salt and freshly-ground black pepper

½ cup dried French green lentils*

1 bay leaf (preferably Turkish)

3 cups cool water

4 cups baby spinach, washed

½ small red onion, thinly sliced

POMEGRANATE VINAIGRETTE

¼ cup pomegranate juice

1 Tablespoon red wine vinegar

2 teaspoons shallot, minced

½ teaspoon Dijon mustard

1 Tablespoon honey, or to taste

⅓ cup extra virgin olive oil

salt and freshly-ground black pepper

Preheat the oven to 425°F. Line a baking sheet with aluminum foil or parchment paper. Place the sweet potatoes in a medium mixing bowl and toss with the oil; season generously with salt and pepper. Arrange the sweet potatoes on the lined baking sheet, spreading to make an even layer. Roast until the potatoes are slightly browned and tender when pierced with a skewer or the tip of a small knife, about 30 minutes. Hold warm in a 200°F oven until needed.

Pick over the lentils, removing any debris or shriveled lentils; rinse, and drain. Combine the lentils, bay leaf and 3 cups of water in a medium saucepan with a tight fitting lid; cover the pan. Bring to the boil, then reduce the heat and simmer, uncovered, until the lentils are just tender, about 20 to 25 minutes. Drain the lentils, and discard the bay leaf. Set aside until needed.

For the dressing, combine the pomegranate juice, vinegar, shallot, mustard and honey in a medium mixing bowl. Add the oil in a slow steady stream, whisking constantly and vigorously, until the dressing is creamy and thoroughly combined (emulsified). Taste, and adjust the seasoning as needed with salt, pepper and honey; set aside until needed.

To serve, place the vinaigrette in a small sauté pan over low heat; cook just to warm through, about 2 to 3 minutes; whisk again just before adding to the salad. Toss the spinach and lentils with the warm vinaigrette, then season to taste with salt and pepper. Mound onto warm individual salad plates, then add the onions and warm sweet potatoes over each salad; serve immediately.

* ½ cup dried lentils yields 1 to 1 ¼ cup cooked lentils.

So many great flavors going on in this salad!

Kathy Woodliff via the Viking Cooking School

JANE ANN'S SPINACH SALAD

2 bags of spinach

6 pieces of bacon

½ cup Jarlsberg cheese

¼ cup or more walnuts

DRESSING

½ cup sugar

½ cup white vinegar

2 Tablespoons salad oil

1 Tablespoon green onions, thinly sliced

1 Tablespoon parsley, snipped

1 teaspoon Worcestershire sauce

1 teaspoon prepared mustard (may use Dijon)

cracked black pepper

Shake in dressing bottle or whisk in a bowl. Cover and chill for 1 hour. Dress salad just before serving.

This is my go-to salad. It is great with filet or brisket.

Jane Ann Moore

SUMMER ARUGULA SALAD

Serves 6

4 cups baby arugula leaves

4 cups curly green leaf lettuce or baby spinach

1 ripe mango, cubed

1 cup fresh blueberries

¼ cup chopped red onion, optional

DRESSING

½ cup extra virgin olive oil

¼ cup lemon juice

2 teaspoons white wine vinegar

¼ teaspoon sea salt

¼ teaspoon garlic, finely chopped

⅛ teaspoon freshly-ground black pepper

Combine salad ingredients in a large bowl. Whisk together the dressing ingredients, and toss with salad ingredients just before serving. Another dressing option is Ume Balsamic Dressing from Rainbow Grocery.

Annie Laurie McRee

ARUGULA *with* ROASTED PEARS AND GOAT CHEESE

Serves 4-6

- 2 Tablespoons unsalted butter, melted
- 2 or 3 firm Bosc pears, halved lengthwise and cored
- sea salt and freshly-ground black pepper
- 4-6 cups baby arugula
- 1 Tablespoon sherry or balsamic vinegar
- 2 Tablespoons olive oil
- 4-6 ounces goat cheese at room temperature
- ¼ cup honey

Preheat oven to 400. Brush a baking sheet with some of the melted butter.

To roast the pears, arrange the pear halves, cut sides down, on a buttered sheet. Brush tops with remaining butter. Season with salt and pepper. Roast until just tender to the point of a knife, 20 to 25 minutes.

To dress the greens, place the arugula in a large bowl. Drizzle with vinegar and olive oil. Season with salt and pepper and toss to combine and coat.

To serve, divide greens among 4 to 6 individual serving plates. Top each with a warm roasted pear half, cut side up. Place a spoonful of goat cheese on each pear. Drizzle with honey.

Sometimes I add roasted walnuts or pecans and dried cranberries.

👑 Susan Johnson from *Bon Appétit Y'all*
by Virginia Willis and Ellen Silverman

ORANGE, DATE AND ARUGULA SALAD *with* ALMONDS

Serves 10

- 10 cups baby arugula
- 3 Tablespoons almond oil or olive oil, divided
- 1 teaspoon fresh lemon juice
- 4 large oranges, peeled, cut crosswise into ⅓-inch-thick rounds
- 15 Medjool dates, halved, pitted
- 1 small wedge Parmesan cheese, shaved
- ½ cup almonds, coarsely chopped

Toss arugula, 1 tablespoon oil and lemon juice in large bowl until coated; sprinkle with salt and pepper. Mound arugula on platter or in large shallow dish and top with orange rounds, dates and Parmesan cheese. Drizzle remaining 2 tablespoons oil over salad, sprinkle with almonds and serve.

👑 Susan Johnson

FRESH HERB SALAD

Serves 4

½ (packed) cup fresh basil leaves,
  torn in half if very large

¼ (packed) cup fresh flat-leaf parsley

2 cups baby mache (or baby arugula or mesclun
  or micro greens)

lemon zest

LEMON-HONEY VINAIGRETTE

1 large lemon

¼ cup fresh lemon juice (about 1½ lemons)

1 Tablespoon honey, or to taste

½ teaspoon kosher salt, or to taste

½ teaspoon freshly-ground black pepper,
  or to taste

¼ cup extra virgin olive oil

Finely zest the lemon, and set aside until needed.
(One lemon should yield 2 to 3 teaspoons of zest.)
Combine the lemon juice, honey, salt and pepper in a
blender or mini food processor. With the motor running, slowly drizzle in the olive oil until the mixture is
smooth and creamy; taste and adjust the seasoning
as needed with salt, pepper and honey.

   Place the basil, parsley, mache and lemon zest
in a salad bowl; toss with just enough vinaigrette to
lightly coat, then season to taste with salt and pepper.
Serve immediately, offering additional freshly-ground
black pepper, if desired.

This dressing is so fresh and simple!

Kathy Woodliff via the Viking Cooking School

BEET, ARUGULA, MINT AND GOAT CHEESE SALAD

Serves 4

10 small beets, trimmed

¼ cup olive oil

3 Tablespoons fresh lemon juice

1 large clove of garlic, minced

Salt and pepper to taste

1 Tablespoon fresh mint, chopped

10 cups arugula leaves

4 dozen fresh mint leaves, whole

⅔ cup goat cheese, crumbled

Wrap the beets in foil. Bake at 350° for 1 hour or until
tender. Let stand until cool. Peel the beets and cut
into thin slices.

   Whisk the olive oil, lemon juice and garlic in a
small bowl. Season with salt and pepper.

   Combine the beets, chopped mint and 2 tablespoons of the dressing in a bowl and toss until the
beets are well-coated.

   Combine the arugula and whole mint leaves in a
large bowl. Add the remaining dressing and toss until
well-coated. Arrange on a serving platter. Top greens
with the beet mixture. Sprinkle with goat cheese.
Serve immediately.

Phoebe Pearigin from *Bay Tables*
by the Junior League of Mobile, Inc.

ARUGULA SALAD with LEMON-PARMESAN DRESSING

4 cups (packed) baby arugula

1 cup halved cherry tomatoes

LEMON-PARMESAN DRESSING

⅓ cup Parmesan cheese, freshly-grated

5 Tablespoons extra virgin olive oil

2 Tablespoons fresh lemon juice

1 teaspoon lemon peel, finely grated

salt and pepper to taste

Blend dressing ingredients in food processor. Season with salt and pepper. Transfer to bowl. Cover and chill up to 3 days.

To serve, combine arugula and tomatoes in large bowl. Toss with enough dressing to coat.

Emmie King

BEVERLY'S ARUGULA SALAD

4-6 servings

1 (1.5-pound) container of baby arugula

3 Tablespoons Champagne vinegar

¼ teaspoon sea salt

⅛ teaspoon freshly-ground pepper

3 Tablespoons olive oil (We use citron-flavored from O & Co.)

Pecorino Romano cheese

Whisk together vinegar, salt and pepper. Let sit for 5 minutes. Then continue whisking while you drizzle in the olive oil. Shave block of pecorino with vegetable peeler. Toss arugula with dressing and shaved pecorino, reserving a few pieces to put on top.

Beverly Painter

ARUGULA AND ENDIVE SALAD

1 package baby arugula

2 heads of endive (ok to use arugula only)

Juice of 1 lemon

sea salt, freshly-ground black pepper

extra virgin olive oil

freshly-shaved Parmesan

Place greens in a bowl (endive halved, core removed, and sliced diagonally). Sprinkle with salt and pepper, squeeze lemon juice over it, drizzle with olive oil, toss, place cheese on top, serve immediately.

Beverly Fulcher

ASPARAGUS VINAIGRETTE

Fresh asparagus

LA MARTINIQUE VINAIGRETTE

Vinegar (red wine, white, or apple cider)

Dijon mustard

Lemon juice

Blanche asparagus in boiling water for 3 minutes, then drain and pour into a bowl of ice water to stop the cooking.

Mix the asparagus with the dressing and marinate for an hour or so before serving. Can be served chilled or at room temperature.

Dorothy Hawkins

ARTICHOKE AND HEARTS OF PALM SALAD

Serves 20

- 3 (10-12 count) cans artichoke hearts, drained
- 3 cans hearts of palm, drained
- 3 small cans sliced black olives, drained
- 3 small (or 2 medium) jars of sliced mushrooms
- 1 large jar (or two small) diced pimientos, drained on paper towels

Slice the artichoke hearts and hearts of palm horizontally into thin slices. Combine all ingredients in a plastic container or Ziploc bag, so you can marinate the salad overnight.

DRESSING

- 1 cup good olive oil
- ½ cup salad or red wine vinegar
- ½ teaspoon tarragon
- ½ teaspoon oregano
- ¼ cup lemon juice
- 2 Tablespoons Worcestershire
- 2 Tablespoons Dijon mustard (can use the coarse grind if necessary)

Mix all dressing ingredients—I like to use my hand blender to really emulsify it. Saturate the vegetables and refrigerate overnight.

This is yummy and keeps a long time in the fridge.

 Jane Alexander, adapted from *The Jackson Cookbook*

LeFLEUR'S BLUFF SALAD

- 1 can hearts of palm, cut in strips
- 1 can artichoke hearts, sliced
- 3 boiled eggs, chopped
- 10 slices bacon, fried and crumbled
- 4 scallions, chopped
- 10 cups lettuce, torn

DRESSING

- 1 clove garlic, minced
- 1 cup mayonnaise
- 1 teaspoon mustard
- ½ cup salad oil
- 1 teaspoon Worcestershire
- 1 teaspoon black pepper
- 1 teaspoon paprika
- ½ cup onion, grated
- 1 Tablespoon water
- Tabasco to taste
- salt to taste

Mix all dressing ingredients in a blender. Refrigerate at least one hour. Toss greens in a large bowl with sufficient dressing to coat. Combine the hearts of palm and artichoke hearts and toss with dressing. Layer greens, palm and artichoke mixture and top with egg, bacon, and scallions.

Claire Barksdale

BROCCOLI SALAD

Serves 6-8

3-5 cups broccoli florets

8-12 slices bacon, cooked and crumbled (I use
Oscar Mayer Real Bacon Pieces)

½ cup purple onion, chopped

¼ cup shelled sunflower seeds, I use more

½-1 cup extra-sharp cheddar, grated

8 green onions, white and green parts chopped

2 avocados

dried cranberries, I use a bunch

DRESSING

juice of 1 lemon

Hidden Valley Ranch dressing

Mix salad ingredients and add dressing. I squeeze the juice of a great big squishy lemon (roll it first on the countertop so it will release juice, cut it and squeeze through cheesecloth or your hand to catch seeds), then I mix it with some Hidden Valley Ranch dressing (this dressing is rather thick, so you might want even a little more lemon juice) and stir. Stir in enough to get the right color—not too white or you have too much dressing. Try maybe ⅓ of a big bottle—you need to be able to see the ingredients, not a big amorphous blob of white stuff. I originally put about that much, and then had to add another couple of cups of broccoli and stir like the dickens to mix it all and get the right color. The point is to be able to taste all the cheese, bacon, both onions, seeds, avocado, dried cranberries and broccoli, and not just the dressing.

👑 Margaret Tohill

BELINDA'S BROCCOLI SALAD

2 heads broccoli—just the florets, cut in bite-size pieces

½ cup salted sunflower seeds

½ cup white raisins

½ cup purple onion, diced

1 box grape tomatoes, halved

3 ounces Real Bacon Bits

DRESSING

1 cup Hellman's mayonnaise

½ cup sugar

2 Tablespoons white vinegar

Mix dressing, then toss with everything else.

 Betty Allin

MAKE-AHEAD AVOCADO SALAD

3 Haas avocados, peeled, pitted and tossed in lemon juice

3 medium tomatoes, sliced

½ of a red onion, thinly sliced

½ cup fresh basil, thinly sliced

4 ounces feta cheese, crumbled

12 ounces mixed salad greens

VINAIGRETTE

¾ cup olive oil

¼ cup white wine vinegar

1 large shallot, minced

salt and pepper to taste

Layer in a glass casserole dish the avocado, tomatoes, onion, basil and cheese.

Whisk together vinaigrette ingredients and pour over the layers. Chill for 3-4 hours.

To serve, toss everything with about 12 ounces mixed salad greens.

Lisa Ireland

COLD CORN SALAD

3 cans of white shoe peg corn, drained
1 cucumber, peeled and chopped
3 bunches of green onions, chopped
1 carton of grape tomatoes, cut in half
mayonnaise to taste
cayenne red pepper to taste
salt and pepper to taste

Mix all ingredients and chill. Serve as a salad or a dip.

Weegie Harris

MARINATED CORN AND BEAN SALAD

¾ cup sugar
¾ cup vinegar
½ cup vegetable oil
1 Tablespoon water
1 teaspoon pepper
½ teaspoon salt
1 (16-ounce can) French style beans, drained
1 (16-ounce can) English peas, drained
1 (17-ounce can) whole kernel corn, drained
1 cup onion, chopped
1 cup green pepper, chopped
1 jar pimento

Combine first 6 ingredients in small saucepan. Bring to a boil. Remove from heat; cool. Place remaining ingredients in a large bowl. Pour vinegar mixture over vegetables. Cover and chill at least 4 hours. Serve with a slotted spoon.

Rachel Misener from her mother, Sharon Busler

CHARRED CORN SALAD

4 cobs fresh corn

Extra virgin olive oil for brushing

1 large garlic clove, minced

1 teaspoon fresh ginger, grated

2 Tablespoons fresh lime juice

1 Tablespoon apple cider vinegar

1 teaspoon honey

2 Tablespoons extra virgin olive oil

sea salt and freshly-ground pepper

1 sweet red or orange bell pepper, diced

1 firm but ripe avocado, pitted, peeled and chopped (prepare just before serving)

1 jalapeno pepper, seeded and finely chopped

2 green onions, finely chopped

2 Tablespoons fresh cilantro or flat-leaf parsley, chopped

1 Tablespoon fresh mint, chopped

Preheat grill to medium-high. Shuck corn, brush with olive oil and cook for 12 to 15 minutes, until golden brown on all sides. Remove from heat and let cool.

Combine garlic, ginger, lime juice, vinegar and honey in a large serving bowl. Gradually whisk in olive oil, and season with salt and pepper to taste. Set aside.

Cut kernels off corn cobs with a serrated knife and add to the dressing. Add red pepper, avocado, jalapeno, green onions, cilantro and mint to the corn. Toss to combine. Serve at room temperature or chilled.

Great summer dish!

Kathy Woodliff

COUNTRY CUCUMBER SALAD

4 cucumbers, peeled and sliced

1 Tablespoon salt

½ teaspoon pepper

½ cup sour cream

3 Tablespoon tarragon vinegar

1 Tablespoon sugar

1 teaspoon paprika

3 Tablespoons chives, minced

2 heads Boston lettuce

Sprinkle cucumbers with salt and refrigerate for 10 minutes. Sprinkle cucumbers with pepper. Mix together sour cream, vinegar and sugar. Pour over cucumbers. Serve in individual servings over Boston lettuce leaves. Sprinkle with paprika and chives.

Walterine Odom

CUCUMBER SALAD

2 cucumbers, peeled and sliced

1 red onion, thinly sliced

Red chili flakes to taste

3 Tablespoons sugar

3 Tablespoons rice wine vinegar

½ cup warm water

Mix all ingredients and refrigerate.

Kathryn McCraney

LIBBA'S MARINATED CUCUMBERS

4 medium cucumbers

2 small Vidalia onions

½ cup white vinegar

¼ cup sugar (I use equivalent Splenda)

½ teaspoon salt

big dash of black pepper

3 Tablespoons fresh dill, finely chopped

Slice cucumbers and onions very thin. I use a mandoline. Mix sweetener, vinegar, salt, pepper and dill very well. Pour over cucumber and onion and chill at least 2 hours. Better the next day.

I add more dill because I love fresh dill—delish! If you use dry dill, use less.

Libba Wilkes

GREEN BEAN SALAD

Serves 12

½ cup sugar

1 cup Wesson oil

1 cup apple cider vinegar

2 cloves garlic, chopped

1 Tablespoon salt

4 (14 ½-ounce) cans whole green beans, drained and washed

2 cans artichoke hearts, drained and cut

Mix marinade with hand mixer and pour over beans and artichokes. Refrigerate overnight.

Meredith May

SUGAR SNAP SALAD

Serves 4

1 Tablespoon fresh lime juice

1 teaspoon fresh ginger, grated

1 Tablespoon olive oil

¼ teaspoon Kosher salt

¼ teaspoon black pepper

4 cups sugar snap peas, strings removed*

1 small red onion, thinly sliced

1 Tablespoon sesame seeds, toasted (optional)

In a large bowl, combine the lime juice, ginger, oil, salt and pepper. Add the snap peas, onion and sesame seeds. Toss to coat.

   *Taste the sugar snaps before making the salad. If they are not as sweet as you'd like, steam them for a minute or two, then run them under cold water. This will help bring out their natural sugars and make them more tender.

JoAnne Prichard Morris

PAINTER'S LADY PEA SALAD

8-10 servings

1½ pounds lady peas

2 cans chicken stock

ham hock

1 yellow bell pepper

1 red bell pepper

1 red onion

3-4 cloves garlic, minced

3 Tablespoons white wine vinegar

2 Tablespoons balsamic vinegar

3 Tablespoons olive oil

2 Tablespoons lemon juice

salt and pepper

Cook peas in chicken stock and 2 cups water with ham hock for approximately 30 minutes (should still be firm). Drain and cool slightly. Dice peppers and onion and mix with cooled peas. Add minced garlic, vinegars, lemon juice and oil. Salt and pepper to taste. Serve cold.

Beverly Painter

PETIT POIS A LA FRANCAISE

2 Tablespoons butter

12 pearl onions, peeled

1 teaspoon sugar

¼ cup pancetta, cut into small pieces

1 Tablespoon olive oil

4 cups fresh peas, shelled

1 Romaine lettuce, cut into pieces

sea salt

freshly-ground black pepper

Bring a small saucepan of water to a boil. Melt the butter in another small saucepan over medium heat. When it is foaming, throw in the onions and cook 4 to 5 minutes, stirring occasionally, without browning. Season with salt and pepper, then add enough water to cover the onions and cook 15 minutes, or until the onions are soft and the liquid reduces by half. Add the sugar and cook, stirring, 3 to 4 minutes until the onions are glazed, transparent and shiny, then set aside.

Add the pancetta to the pan of boiling water and blanch 1 to 2 minutes, then refresh in cold water, drain and pat dry. Heat the oil in a skillet over medium heat and sauté the pancetta 7 to 8 minutes until crisp and golden brown, then set aside.

Add the peas and Romaine lettuce to the pan with the onions and simmer, stirring occasionally, 3 to 4 minutes. The peas should be tender, the onions still whole and the lettuce just a little crunchy. Add the pancetta and season with salt and pepper. Serve hot.

Holly Wagner

MARINATED YELLOW SQUASH

4-6 very small squash (I don't go by this; I just buy the amount I think I will need which is usually a lot more)

⅓ cup salt

1 cup purple onion, chopped fine

1 cup bell pepper, chopped fine

1 jar pimiento, chopped (I also chop up red bell pepper for crunch and more color)

¾ cup sugar

1 cup white vinegar

1 Tablespoon mustard seed

Slice squash very thinly (almost wafer thin) into 1-½ quarts cold water in which the salt has been added. Refrigerate overnight.

Drain. Add onion, red and green bell peppers, and pimiento to squash.

Boil sugar, vinegar, and mustard seed. Pour hot mixture over vegetables. Refrigerate, covered, overnight.

Mary Delle McCarthy, adapted from *Southern Accents*, the Junior League of Pine Bluff, Arkansas, cookbook—an excellent cookbook, I might add!

FRESH CHERRY TOMATO SALAD

Serves 8 to 10

2 pints cherry tomatoes, sliced in half

2 pints yellow pear tomatoes, sliced in half

1 cup green onions, thinly sliced

½ cup goat's milk feta cheese, crumbled

2 Tablespoons cilantro, chopped

salt and pepper, to taste

½ cup extra virgin olive oil

4 Tablespoons cider vinegar

½ cup pine nuts, toasted

Mix all ingredients except pine nuts in a bowl until well combined. Add pine nuts just before serving.

Sue Allen Tate from *Square Table* by the Yoknapatawpha Arts Council, Oxford, Mississippi

MAMA'S STUFFED TOMATOES

garden fresh summer tomatoes

saltine crackers (crushed)

Lee and Perrin's Worcestershire sauce

store-bought mayonnaise

salt and fresh-ground black pepper

Scoop out the insides of the ripe tomatoes into a mixing bowl, leaving enough tomato so that they hold their shape.

Add crushed saltines, mayonnaise, and salt and pepper to taste. Refill the tomatoes and place on bed of lettuce for a simple and delightful summer salad or quick lunch. Serve with more fresh saltines.

This is a perfect use for those extra tomatoes that need to be eaten. And if you are as lazy as I am, it tastes just as good eaten straight out of the bowl!

Mary Arrington Jones

TOMATO PIE

fresh tomatoes

sugar

tarragon

basil

onion, diced

bell pepper, diced

1 cup mild cheddar cheese, shredded

1½ cups mayonnaise

soda crackers

Place two layers of tomatoes in bottom of casserole; sprinkle with sugar, tarragon and basil. Add onion and bell pepper. Combine cheese and mayonnaise; spread over all. Crumble soda crackers on top.

Bake in 350° oven for 30 to 40 minutes.

Marjorie Underwood

BASIL TOMATO SALAD

2 large cucumbers, sliced in ¼-inch rounds

4 large ripe tomatoes, sliced in ½-inch rounds

1 sweet red onion, peeled and sliced in ⅛-inch rounds

½ bunch (handful) fresh basil

1½ cups rice vinegar

salt, pepper and olive oil

Stem basil, wash and pat dry. Chop half of basil leaves coarsely. Reserve remainder for garnish.

Arrange onion, tomatoes and cucumber slices in serving bowl. Sprinkle with chopped basil; pour vinegar over ingredients. Cover and refrigerate at least 3 hours, preferably overnight.

Before serving, drain off most of the liquid and discard. Garnish with remaining basil. Add salt, pepper and drizzle of olive oil and serve chilled.

Donna Barksdale

WINIFRED'S TOMATO ASPIC

Serves 8

3 cups tomato juice

2 envelopes unflavored gelatin

¼ cup cold water

1 teaspoon salt

1 teaspoon sugar

1 teaspoon green onion, chopped

1 teaspoon parsley, chopped

2 teaspoons Worcestershire sauce

1 Tablespoon onion juice or 1 teaspoon onion, pureed

4 drops Tabasco

2 teaspoons lemon juice

1 Tablespoon prepared horseradish

½ cup celery, finely chopped

½ cup stuffed olives, sliced

1 avocado, cut into chunks, or 1 (14-ounce) can artichoke hearts, drained and washed

boiled shrimp, cut small, optional

Lightly grease a 2-quart baking dish. Dissolve gelatin in cold water. Bring tomato juice to a boil and remove from heat. Stir in gelatin, salt, sugar, green onion and parsley. Let cool, then add remaining ingredients; pour into baking dish and chill.

The garden club has had this tomato aspic from Winifred Green Cheney several times and it is a great recipe.

Susan Shands Jones

ELLY LAUNIUS' MYSTERY SALAD

3 (3-ounce) packages raspberry gelatin

1½ cups hot water

3 cans Italian stewed tomatoes

6 drops Tabasco

Dissolve gelatin in hot water. Stir in tomatoes, breaking with a spoon, if you wish. Add Tabasco and stir. Pour into your favorite lightly oiled 12-cup ring mold. Chill until firm. Unmold on greens and serve with a dressing of horseradish and light mayonnaise.

This recipe called for a can of plain stewed tomatoes. I switched to the Italian version at godchild Jane Alexander's suggestion. I also use sugar-free Jell-O to keep the caloric content down for family and friends who say it's their favorite congealed salad.

Barbara Austin via *The Jackson Cookbook*

BLOODY MARY TOMATO ASPIC

Serves 8

½ bottle Zing Zang Bloody Mary mix

1 (12-ounce) can V-8 juice

2 Tablespoons horseradish

1 Tablespoon lime juice

½ cup pimento-stuffed green olives, finely chopped

½ cup green onions, finely chopped

½ cup celery, finely chopped

4 envelopes unflavored gelatin

½ cup cold water

small shrimp or crabmeat, optional

Combine first 7 ingredients and put over low heat to meld flavors for 10 minutes. While liquids are heating, dissolve gelatin in cold water, then add to heated liquids stirring constantly for about 1 minute. Remove from heat and pour into individual molds or ring mold. If you want to speed up the congealing process, pour liquid aspic into metal or glass bowl and put bowl into ice bath.

Small shrimp or crabmeat can be added to final mix or put around congealed aspic, if desired

Buddie Barksdale via her sister,
Melanie Williams

ELLEN'S TOMATO ASPIC

40 ounces canned tomato juice or V-8

2 dashes of Worcestershire

1 whole lemon, quartered

1 small onion, quartered

1 teaspoon cloves

2 stalks celery

2 bay leaves

1 teaspoon parsley flakes

1 teaspoon sugar

1 teaspoon salt

1 dash Tabasco

1 can Campbell's beef consomme'

1 envelope unflavored gelatin

2 stalks celery

1 small jar salad olives

1 small can artichoke heart

Simmer first 12 ingredients for 10 minutes and strain. Just juice will remain. Add 1 envelope of gelatin to 2 scant cups of juice. Use individual molds or a large Bundt pan. If using a Bundt pan, spray the bottom with Pam.

Cut up celery, olives and artichoke hearts to cover bottom of molds or Bundt pan. Pour juice over. Refrigerate until set or firm.

Ellen Treadway

VIRGINIA'S TOMATO ASPIC

1 box lemon Jell-O

1 (14.5-ounce) can stewed tomatoes

a few drops of Tabasco

a few drops of Worcestershire sauce

1 package spring mix

mayonnaise

fresh dill

Drain stewed tomatoes well and reserve juice. Prepare lemon Jell-O according to directions. Add enough cold water to reserved tomato juice to make one cup and use this instead of plain water.

Add a few drops each of Tabasco and Worcestershire sauce to Jell-O mixture, more if you like it spicy. Add stewed tomatoes. Stir very well. Refrigerate 4 hours or until firm.

Topping (if you wish to have one): mayonnaise with fresh dill. Serve on a bed of spring mix.

Virginia Farr

FROZEN TOMATOES

1 large can tomato juice

2 small cans tomato juice

1½ packages unflavored gelatin

lemon juice

onion juice

Worcestershire sauce

salt and pepper

1½ cups mayonnaise, approximately

Season tomato juice with lemon juice, onion juice, Worcestershire sauce, salt and pepper to taste. Heat slightly to dissolve gelatin which has been softened with a little water. Mix in mayonnaise. Put in ice cream freezer and freeze. Transfer to container and keep in freezer.

This was my grandmother, Mrs. Webster Buie's, recipe.

Marjorie Underwood

SIPPABLE SALAD, *aka* GAZPACHO

6 large ripe tomatoes

2 sweet red bell peppers

2 medium Vidalia onions

2 large cucumbers

1 tart apple (such as Granny Smith), peeled and cored

2 garlic cloves, minced

½ cup red wine vinegar

½ cup olive oil

2 cups spicy V-8 or tomato juice

1 cup chicken broth

Pinch of cayenne pepper

Salt and pepper

Wash and chop the vegetables and apple in a food processor. It may be necessary to chop in small batches. I prefer the vegetables to be coarsely chopped, but they can be pureed if you prefer.

In a small bowl whisk together vinegar and olive oil, then mix with chopped vegetables, broth and seasonings in large covered bowl or pitcher. Chill for at least four hours.

Serve in chilled soup bowls or mugs.

If the gazpacho is kept for several days it may be necessary to add additional V-8 juice for desired consistency.

Judy Wiener

FRESH FENNEL, GREEN BEAN AND TOMATO SALAD

Serves 6

6 Tablespoons red wine vinegar

1 Tablespoons Dijon mustard

½ pound green beans, cut into 1½-inch diagonal pieces

2 small or one large fennel bulb (about 1½ pounds)

¾ cups olive oil

¾ cup walnut halves or large pieces

3 cloves garlic, minced

3 cups Italian cherry tomatoes, halved

⅓ cup fresh basil, chopped

salt and pepper

2 heads Boston or butter lettuce, leaves washed and separated for serving

In a small bowl, whisk together vinegar and mustard. Fill a medium saucepan with water, bring to a boil and cook the green beans 1 minute; drain and run under cold water. Cut a thin slice off top and root and of fennel and discard. Slice the bulb into ¼-inch thick slices and then into 1-inch pieces. You should have about 2 cups.

In a large skillet, heat the olive oil over moderate heat; sauté' walnuts until they begin to brown. Add fennel and garlic; cook, stirring constantly, until fennel begins to soften, 2 to 3 minutes. Remove from heat. Stir in tomatoes, green beans, vinegar, mustard and basil. Salt and pepper to taste.

May be held at room temperature for 8 hours or refrigerated overnight; bring to room temperature before serving on lettuce leaves.

Julie Moore

WINDOW SHOP TRINITY

Serves 4-6

- raw beets, grated
- raw carrots, grated
- raw turnips, grated
- dressing of your choice

The vegetables are served in 3 separate stacks on the plate with a choice of dressings. I've tried it with plain vinaigrette, Come Back Dressing, and a vinaigrette with bleu cheese dressing at different times and prefer the plain vinaigrette (I like the flavor of the 3 raw vegetables—personal preference). I imagine other dressings will work as well.

This recipe came by personal experience from the Window Shop on Brattle Street, Cambridge, Massachusetts, when I was a graduate student at Harvard a few decades ago.

I ordered the salad from the menu (don't remember the name of the salad). When it arrived, someone at the next table said: "Oh, you're eating what Julia Child's eating for lunch" and pointed to a woman in the corner of the room. Sure enough, it was Julia Child's choice also. The Window Shop no longer exists, but it was a favorite haunt for many of us at Harvard and in Cambridge, including Julia Child.

I imagine the vegetables Window Shop used were organically grown; I definitely recommend organic today.

Ruth Black

BROCCOLI RAMEN NOODLE COLE SLAW

- 1 (16-ounce) package broccoli cole slaw
- 2 (3-ounce) packages ramen noodles, oriental flavor
- 1 cup sliced almonds
- ¼ cup red wine vinegar
- ⅓ cup sugar
- ½ cup vegetable oil
- 2 packages oriental flavor seasoning (from the soup)

Crumble ramen noodles and combine with broccoli slaw and sliced almonds. Combine red wine vinegar, sugar, vegetable oil, and oriental seasoning. Heat mixture over low heat until sugar and seasoning dissolve. Cool and pour over slaw mixture.

You may add chicken or tuna and use this salad as a main dish.

Jane Roper

ORIENTAL COLE SLAW

1-pound package cole slaw

8 green onions, chopped

1 cup sliced almond

4 Tablespoons sesame seeds

1 package ramen noodles, chicken flavor

¾ cup canola oil

4 Tablespoons apple cider vinegar

4 Tablespoons sugar

1 teaspoon cayenne

Toast almonds and sesame seeds. Combine oil, vinegar, chicken flavor package, sugar, salt and pepper to taste, and cayenne.

Combine chopped green onions with cole slaw. Toss with dressing just before serving.

Add toasted almonds and sesame seeds, along with broken up ramen noodles. Enjoy!

Vicki Swayze

Virginia Ezelle makes this salad with 2 packages ramen noodles, adding only one flavor packet to ½ cup cider vinegar, ½ cup oil, 4 Tablespoons sugar and ½ teaspoon cayenne or a few drops of Tabasco.

WILLIAM'S COLE SLAW

1 package mixed slaw with carrots

1 Granny Smith apple, cut into large chunks

1 package dried cranberries

1 cup toasted pecans, chopped

1 bottle creamy poppy seed dressing

Mix together, chill and serve.

Jan Wofford

ASIAN SLAW

2 bags broccoli slaw

1 cup sliced almonds

4 Tablespoons unsalted butter

1 package ramen noodles, discard flavor packet

SWEET AND SOUR DRESSING

1 cup vegetable oil

1 cup sugar

½ cup wine vinegar

3 teaspoons soy sauce

salt and pepper

Toast almonds and noodles in butter; cool on paper towels. Add to broccoli slaw. Blend dressing ingredients. Toss with salad.

This slaw is a refreshing variation on Come on In*'s* Crunchy Romaine Toss.

Kay Mortimer

WINTER SALAD

Serves 6

2 cups cabbage, finely shredded

½ cup celery, sliced

1 cup carrots, shredded

1 cup Swiss chard, finely shredded

2 Tablespoons parsley, chopped

¼ cup walnuts or toasted pine nuts, chopped

¼ cup pitted Kalamata or green olives, sliced

DRESSING

¼ cup extra virgin olive oil

2 Tablespoons balsamic vinegar

1 Tablespoon soy sauce

½ teaspoon coarsely ground black pepper, or to taste

½ cup Romano cheese, grated

Toss together the cabbage, celery and carrots. Make the dressing and toss into the salad. Chill, covered, for 30 minutes. Before serving, add shredded chard and parsley, and top with the nuts and olives.

Betty Hise via friend Marilyn Harris, long-time Cincinnati radio food show host and a Mississippi native

VON'S PANZANELLA OR TUSCAN BREAD SALAD

Serves 4

13 ounces stale bread (1 loaf of ciabatta from Broad Street works nicely)

1 medium purple onion

1 medium cucumber

6 leaves fresh basil, rolled and sliced or hand-shredded, plus a few extra for garnish.

13 ounces fresh tomatoes, diced, or cherry tomatoes, sliced in half

1 cup fresh or frozen lima beans, blanched and shocked

1 teaspoon red wine vinegar

3 Tablespoons extra virgin olive oil

Kosher or sea salt

freshly-ground pepper

Slice the bread and soak in cold water for about 40 minutes. Meanwhile, slice the onion into pieces (not too small). Set aside. Cut the cucumber into thin slices, sprinkle with salt, cover with a cloth and put a heavy or weighted plate on top to press the liquid from the cucumber for about 10 minutes.

Squeeze the soaked bread with hands, crumble into a large mixing bowl, and set aside. Wash and dry the cucumber.

In a second bowl combine the cucumber, lima beans, onions, tomatoes, and basil leaves. Dress with extra virgin olive oil and stir. Combine the vegetables with the bread and add the vinegar. Add salt, pepper, and more olive oil and vinegar to taste. Let sit 10 minutes so that the flavors can combine, then serve. Alternatively, it can be made several hours ahead of time and refrigerated.

This works nicely formed in a 4-inch circle mold. Garnish with extra basil and olive oil.

Von Jicka from the Badia a Coltibuono cooking school in Chianti, Italy

BEVERLY'S PANZANELLA

Serves 6

1 loaf French bread

1 pint cherry tomatoes, halved

½ red onion, finely chopped

1 English cucumber, sliced and quartered

⅓ cup basil, torn into pieces

¼ cup celery leaves, torn into pieces

1 Tablespoon capers

2 roasted red peppers

DRESSING

2 garlic cloves

3 anchovy fillets

2 teaspoons kosher salt

Freshly ground black pepper

Juice of ½ lemon

2 Tablespoons red wine vinegar

Use a mortar and pestle to make a paste of the salt, garlic, anchovies. Next add the lemon juice, wine vinegar and pepper. Mix and set aside.

Tear bread into 1-inch pieces, sprinkle with sea salt and toss with olive oil, toast in oven on parchment-covered cookie sheet for 10-15 min at 350°.

To roast peppers, cut in half and seed, sprinkle with salt and pepper, rub both sides with olive oil, place on cookie sheet lined with foil, skin side up. Broil until skins are blackened and blistered, place in bowl and seal with plastic wrap to cool, then remove skins and slice peppers.

Toss all ingredients with dressing and top it all with the French bread croutons.

Beverly Fulcher

CORNBREAD SALAD

1 (8½-ounce) package of cornbread muffin mix

1 (1-ounce) envelope Ranch-style dressing mix

1 (8-ounce) container sour cream

1 cup mayonnaise

3 medium tomatoes, chopped

½ cup red bell pepper, chopped

½ cup green bell pepper, chopped

½ cup green onions, chopped

Prepare cornbread mix according to package directions; cool. Stir together salad dressing mix, sour cream and mayonnaise until blended; set aside. Combine tomatoes and next 3 ingredients and gently toss. Crumble half the cornbread into a 3-quart trifle bowl or large salad bowl. Layer tomato mixture and dressing mixture; repeat layers. Cover and chill 3 hours.

Ellen Treadway

Dressings

(See the Salad Dressing Index in the back of this book for a complete listing of all dressings.)

AUNT CARA'S HONEY TARRAGON DRESSING

½ cup seasoned rice vinegar

¼ cup canola oil or vegetable oil

¼ cup honey

splash of water

2 cloves garlic, crushed

1 teaspoon tarragon

This is a good summertime salad dressing. Light, cool and sweet.

♔ Anne Robertson

DELICIOUS DRESSING

Apple cider vinegar

Coconut Oil

Honey

Mix equal parts of each ingredient.

It's delicious!

Jona Keeton

MY MOTHER'S FRENCH DRESSING

½ teaspoon salt

½ teaspoon dry mustard

½ teaspoon paprika

2 Tablespoons lemon juice

2 Tablespoons vinegar

½ cup salad oil

dash of red pepper

Put ingredients in bottle; cover and shake well before using.

Joanne Lyell

GREEK SALAD DRESSING

1 Tablespoon fresh lemon juice

2 Tablespoons good olive oil

¼ teaspoon fresh dill

¼ teaspoon mint

¼ teaspoon minced garlic (can use more, to taste)

¼ teaspoon oregano

¼ teaspoon each salt and pepper

Shake in jar. Use with salad of good lettuce, tomatoes, ripe olives, green onions, cucumbers and feta cheese to taste.

Might as well spread the word about a great kitchen gadget—Zyliss garlic press is the best. Takes the peel off at same time as it minces, one clove at a time. Just checked online—Zyliss garlic press can be had for as little as $7. And there's even a JUMBO size that will press more than one clove at a time. I may have to order that!!! It's fabulous because you don't have to peel the garlic cloves.

Ginnie Munford

LEMON AND BASIL VINAIGRETTE

¼ cup fresh lemon juice

2 teaspoons sugar

2 Tablespoons mayonnaise

½ cup olive oil

½ cup fresh basil

Combine all ingredients in a blender and blend until smooth. This can be made a day in advance and refrigerated.

Virginia Farr

MY GRANDMOTHER'S SALAD DRESSING

½ cup olive oil

4 ½ teaspoons fresh lemon juice

2 teaspoons Dijon mustard

1 Tablespoon onion, grated

2 Tablespoons white wine vinegar

1 teaspoon salt

½ teaspoon pepper

Mix really well—Delish!!!

This recipe is from my grandmother in Greenville, Polly Mock, who is the best cook ever!

Jane Anna Barksdale

OUR FAVORITE DRESSING

2 teaspoons vinegar

1 teaspoon Harvest Course Ground Grey Poupon
    with whole mustard seeds

1 clove garlic, pressed

½ cup olive oil, can adjust to your taste

juice of one lemon

salt and pepper

Let the garlic sit in the vinegar and mustard for a few minutes. Add olive oil, lemon juice, salt and pepper. Toss with fresh greens, tomatoes and avocado. I usually squeeze more lemon juice over the bowl of greens.

Margee Wohner

SIMPLE SALAD DRESSING

Lemons

Lemon infused olive oil
    (regular olive oil may be substituted)

Salt

Squeeze the juice from two lemons and taste the juice of the lemons. If the lemons are very tart use equal parts of lemon juice and lemon infused olive oil. If the lemons are not tart use two parts lemon juice to one part olive oil. Mix lemon juice, olive oil and salt to taste in a bowl and whip—toss with salad and enjoy!

Tastes like summer!

Merrill Tenney McKewen, aka MO

COMEBACK SAUCE

2 cups Dukes mayonnaise

1 cup Hunts ketchup (no high fructose corn syrup)

1 cup chili sauce

1 cup canola oil

1 teaspoon extra virgin olive oil

1 large onion, diced

juice from 1½ lemons

4 cloves garlic, minced

2 Tablespoons Hungarian paprika

2 Tablespoons water

2 Tablespoons Lea and Perrin's Worcestershire sauce

1 Tablespoon freshly-ground black pepper

2 teaspoons dry mustard

⅛ teaspoon celery seed

dash of hot sauce

2 teaspoons sea salt

Puree all ingredients in a food processor. Allow to sit refrigerated for several hours before use.

Del Harrington

WASABI SOY YUM DRESSING

2½ cups mayonnaise

½ cup soy sauce

¼ cup olive oil

½ cup onion, chopped

¼ cup or less of brown sugar

½ Tablespoon stone ground mustard

¼ Tablespoon dry mustard

1 Tablespoon horseradish

Mix together, blend well.

Durden Moss via Penland School of Crafts in North Carolina

TZATZIKI SAUCE

4 cups plain Greek yogurt

8 cups sour cream

4 ounces olive oil

2 ounces lemon juice

1 Tablespoon black pepper

2 Tablespoons garlic, minced

2 Tablespoons garlic powder

2 Tablespoons Cavender's Greek Seasoning

4 teaspoons salt

3 cucumbers, peeled, seeded and minced

Mix all the ingredients with a wire whisk, except cucumbers. Then add the cucumbers. Once fully mixed, the sauce is ready to serve as a side with vegetables or pita bread.

Dorothy Hawkins

Sips

MARGARITA CLASSICA

Serves 1

- 1 ounce freshly-squeezed lime juice (no substitution)
- 1 ounce Triple Sec (better brand)
- 1½ ounce Tequila (Blue Agave certified)

Chill a cocktail glass. Rub the rim with a piece of lime rind remaining from squeezing the fresh limes. Dip rim in finely ground Kosher salt, fill with ice cubes, and pour mixed ingredients over the ice. Garnish with a lime rind twist, and serve.

This is a truly memorable cocktail; just ask anyone attending the spring party when Overton and I prepared quantities of the libation for members and guests, and mis-proportioned the ingredients. We brought the recipe home from Guanajuato, Mexico. Una margarita por favor, y no mas.

Marilyn Moore

GARDEN CLUB 2002 MOJITOS

Serves 16

- 2 packed cups fresh mint
- 1 ⅓ cups sugar
- 1 ⅓ cups fresh lime juice (about 18 large limes)
- 4 cups light rum
- ice cubes
- 3 cups club soda

Combine mint, sugar and lime juice in large bowl; mash well with potato masher. Let stand at least 15 minutes and up to 2 hours. Stir in rum. Using ladle, divide mixture among 16 tall glasses. Fill glasses almost to top with ice cubes, and then top each with 3 tablespoons club soda.

Frances Morrison

CAIPIRINHA

Serves 1

- 1 ⅔ ounce cachaca
- ½ lime cut into 4 wedges
- 2 teaspoons sugar

Place lime and sugar into glass and muddle. Fill glass with crushed ice and the cachaca.

The Caipirinha is the national cocktail of Brazil. Our daughter introduced us to it after attending a wedding in Sao Paulo. It is made with cachaca (sugar cane rum), sugar (preferably raw sugar) and lime.

We were amused to learn that the word caipirinha is derived from the word caipira, which, according to Wikipedia, refers to someone from the countryside. Apparently it is almost the exact equivalent of the American word "hillbilly." It is refreshing but surprisingly potent on a hot summer's day. We make a pitcher by multiplying the quantities. Viva!

Kay Mortimer

WALT'S MANHATTAN

Serves 1

Combine the following in a mixing glass full of ice and STIR until chilled—NEVER SHAKE!!

- 2 ounces rye whiskey
- 1 ounce Italian/sweet vermouth
- 2 dashes of angostura bitters

Garnish with brandied cherries or maraschino cherries.

NEVER BOURBON! NEVER SHAKEN!

Laura Damon Wofford

SEERSUCKER

Serves 1

2 ounces Hendricks Gin

2 ounces honey-thyme syrup

lemon juice

top with club soda

Make a honey-thyme syrup by bringing to a boil equal parts honey and water. Remove from heat, add fresh thyme sprigs and let steep 48 hours. Store in refrigerator.

Kelly Butler from The Snack Bar
in Oxford, Mississippi

BELLINI MARTINI

Serves 1

2 ounces vodka

1 ounce peach nectar or fresh peach juice

½ ounce peach schnapps

Shake over ice, strain and pour. Garnish with mint.

Maribeth Wann

VODKA SLUSH

Serves 12

- 2 large cans frozen lemonade
- 2 large cans water
- 2 small cans frozen limeade
- 2 small cans water
- 1 fifth 100-proof vodka
- Lemon or lime slices (very thin) for garnish

Mix all together, except sliced fruit, and put in freezer; overnight is best. It will turn mushy. That's when it's ready. Garnish each drink with the lemon and lime slices and serve.

Holly Wagner

PEAR BLOSSOM MARTINI

Serves 1

- 2 ounces Grey Goose pear vodka
- ½ ounce lemon-lime soda
- ¾ ounce cranberry juice

Shake with ice, pour into chilled martini glass and garnish with a lemon twist.

Stacy Underwood

BLUEBERRY LEMONADE

1 ounce vodka

½ ounce blueberry syrup

3-4 ounces lemonade (I like Minute Maid Light)

Fresh blueberries

Lemon wedge

Muddle a small handful of blueberries in a glass. Add vodka and blueberry syrup. Add ice. Top off with lemonade—usually 3-4 ounces, but you can adjust however you like. Add lemon wedge and a few fresh blueberries to garnish.

To cut down on calories, you can substitute low calorie blueberry juice for the blueberry syrup and adjust amount for desired sweetness.

Ginger Weaver

SANGRIA BLANCA

Serves 6

½ cup sugar

½ cup fresh lemon juice

1 bottle dry white wine

1 (10 ounce) bottle club soda

½ cup freshly-squeezed orange juice

½ cup Curacao or Grand Marnier

1 lemon, sliced

ice cubes

In a large pitcher, dissolve sugar in lemon juice. Add remaining ingredients and stir well.

Frances Morrison

IN-A-SNAP SANGRIA

Serves 20

- 2 (12-ounce) cans frozen pink lemonade concentrate, thawed and undiluted
- 1 bottle rose wine, chilled
- 1 bottle Burgundy wine, chilled
- juice of 2 limes
- 2 liters club soda, chilled
- 1 lemon, thinly sliced
- 1 lime, thinly sliced
- 1 orange, thinly sliced

Combine first 4 ingredients, mixing well. Slowly stir in club soda. Garnish with fruit slices and serve over ice. This recipe can be made ahead to the point of adding the club soda.

Frances Morrison

BLONDE SANGRIA

Serves 6

- 1 fifth dry white wine
- 1 cup unsweetened pineapple juice
- ⅓ cup orange juice
- 3 Tablespoons lemon juice
- 1 Tablespoon lime juice
- ¼ cup sugar
- 1 cup of 7-Up or Sprite

Mix wine, juices and sugar and chill thoroughly, adding the soda or 7-Up just before serving. Garnish each glass with a cherry, pineapple chunk and orange slice on a toothpick. May be prepared ahead and stored in refrigerator, but do not add soda or 7-Up until serving.

Julie Moore

CRANBERRY SANGRIA

1 quart cranberry juice cocktail

3 cups dry white wine

2½ Tablespoons orange-flavored liqueur
   (Triple Sec)

1 orange, sliced

1 lemon, sliced

1 lime, sliced

1 cup club soda

Mix and chill first six ingredients. Add soda and stir
once to mix. Makes 2 quarts.

Julie Moore via Susan Shands Jones

Salad Dressing Index

Index of Recipes

Additional copies of **SALADS AND SIPS**
may be ordered through

Amazon.com

BarnesandNoble.com

CreateSpace.com/3953059

For wholesale inquiries,
contact CreateSpace Direct at 866-356-2154

Thank you!

NOTES

NOTES

NOTES